N

NATIONAL

S

STUDENT

D

DRAMA

F

FESTIVAL

RAW TALENT

Fifty years of the
N   S   D   F

OBERON BOOKS
LONDON

First published in 2005 by Oberon Books Ltd
521 Caledonian Road, London N7 9RH
Tel 020 7607 3637 Fax 020 7607 3629
oberon.books@btinternet.com
www.oberonbooks.com

ISBN 1 84002 553 0

Printed in Chippenham by Antony Rowe Ltd.

CONTENTS

Special thanks are due to NSDF Patron Sir Alan Ayckbourn for his greatly appreciated continuing support of the National Student Drama Festival.

Whilst we have tried to cover as much as humanly possible of the Festival's history in something that would still be recognisable as a book, it is likely that there will have been omissions, for which I apologise profusely. Similarly, while every attempt has been made at accuracy, it is probable that errors will have crept in. Invaluable in the production of this book have been Tamzin Aitken, Mark Batty, Tash Banks, Dan Bye, Lon David, Alex Ferguson, Robert Hewison, James Hogan, Richard Hurst, Stephen Jeffreys, Barbara Matthews, Sarah Nicholson, Ian Shuttleworth, Dan Steward, Stephen Watson, Chris Wilkinson, Clive and Pat Wolfe. Of course, any mistakes that remain are my own.

Andrew Haydon, 2005

This book has been sponsored by Oberon Books Ltd
and Antony Rowe Ltd

On the evening of Wednesday, 4 January 1956, in the Gentlemen's Toilet of Bristol's Victoria Rooms, I found myself side by side with Harold Hobson, the distinguished drama critic of The Sunday Times. Across the graceful 19th century porcelain divide we talked of the production he had just witnessed of Thornton Wilder's Our Town, which I had directed for the Student Players of Regent Street Polytechnic (now the University of Westminster).

The occasion was the climax of the first ever NUS-organised, Sunday Times-sponsored National Student Drama Festival, and Mr Hobson had just bestowed on our company the trophy for Best Production. We all felt very proud.

Getting the Festival together, selecting from the submitted productions, organising workshops, inviting distinguished professionals to come and talk, to act as judges, to provide technical expertise, had required immense effort on the part of a whole lot of people. Who would have thought, then, that the annual event would survive, burgeon and show no signs of exhaustion, well into the next century?

Probably not the actor who played the pivotal role of Dr Gibbs in my production, Clive Wolfe. It is, however, very much due to Clive's commitment, determination, and, let's face it, personal cash input, that the Festival is now celebrating its fiftieth birthday. Taking the reins from Kenneth Pearson in 1970, Clive continued as NSDF Director until his own retirement in the year 2000.

My conversation with the great drama critic, decorously brief though it was in view of the location, had the effect of determining me to turn down what my father described as a Proper Job, and instead chance my luck in the professional theatre. A defining moment, then, that January evening, in both Clive's life and my own; subsequent Festivals have provided many such moments for a number of people, some of whom today have become household names.

That's not the point, of course. Each year, students of every discipline, every age, every part of the UK (and from abroad, too, sometimes) congregate to devise, perform, speak, witness, learn, discuss, argue, get drunk, write articles for the daily Festival news magazine Noises Off and generally explore the human condition during a hyperactive week in seaside Scarborough.

It's a unique occasion. I'm still involved with the NSDF, and look forward to the celebration each year.

Timothy West

1956, BRISTOL

The mid-1950s were a fertile period for British drama, with landmark events setting the scene for the next fifty years. Two are well known, the premieres of Waiting for Godot and Look Back in Anger. Yet in between these two, though less frequently recorded in the history books, was another theatrical first. It was to prove every bit as influential: the first National Union of Students and Sunday Times Drama Festival, later the National Student Drama Festival or NSDF. This initial Festival was simply a competition for a single award, the Sunday Times Drama Trophy. Finalists were selected from 17 productions entered over the course of the previous year.

The first programme featured an introductory note from the then president of the National Union of Students, Frank Copplestone, explaining the genesis of the Festival:

> It is some years since the National Union of Students organised a festival devoted entirely to drama, but for some time it has been felt that such a festival should be organised, for three main reasons. First, it would provide an opportunity for those students interested in drama to meet, see the best of the current student productions, hear talks on various aspects of the theatre, and join in discussions led by experts. Secondly, it would provide the opportunity for other people to see a selection of university productions, and the present trends of drama among students. Thirdly, since it is hoped that this festival will be the first of a series that will take place annually, we believe that festivals such as this will do much to widen the interest and increase the knowledge of students in drama and its associated arts, and at the same time raise the standard of student productions over the whole country.

The programme also contained an essay from Dr Glynne Wickham entitled 'Drama in the Universities', which described the atmosphere surrounding student drama in the mid-1950s. Wickham was the Winchester- and Oxford-educated great-grandson of Gladstone, and, at the time, head of the only Drama department in the United Kingdom, at the University of Bristol. We might think that theatre studies is a marginalised subject today, and that extra-curricular dramatic activity is not encouraged as much as it might be, but the situation he describes fifty years ago is unimaginably worse.

CHAPTER ONE
CLIVE WOLFE

1956
1959

The *Sunday Times* Trophy

Wickham suggests that there are three main reasons for student interest in drama: 'a convivial relaxation from serious study, a subject of sufficient scope to warrant serious study, or an apprentice-training for a subsequent career'. Few universities, he noted, made any attempt to cater for all three possibilities. They did little more than tolerate interest in drama. Boards of Faculty moaned regularly about too much acting and too little work, their tolerance amounting only to recognising that an interest in drama is a legitimate leisure recreation, while students whose interest was scholarly found it hard to get a specifically theatrical aspect of dramatic studies accepted as a thesis subject. Of the third reason, he observed: 'Only at Oxford or Cambridge (whose proximity to London and long tradition of dramatic performances attracts regular notice from the national press) can a student deliberately use a dramatic society as a stepping stone to a professional career.' Wickham went on to note the vast difference between this situation and that in mainland Europe and America, where 'official tolerance of drama amounts, at the least, to an admission that drama for the world at large is a living art with a substantial history which cuts across several civilisations and consequently merits specialised attentions'. He concluded: 'Drama need not be regarded as mysteriously but necessarily associated with Sin or Neurosis. Nor need the student who decided to take a serious interest in it see himself as regarded by others as a likely sinner or neurotic on that count.' It is odd to reflect that while Beckett and Osborne were breaking the mould of British drama, there was barely any formal opportunity to study theatre as a living art, as opposed to literary text, and involvement in drama itself was viewed as highly suspect.

It was in Bristol, or at least its university and drama department, that the first National Student Drama Festival was held. On the afternoon of New Year's Day, 1956, an apprehensive gaggle of Regent Street Polytechnic students took to the gargantuan stage of the Victoria Halls with a production of Thornton Wilder's Our Town directed by a young Timothy West. For the next three days, each remaining full-length finalist gave a single performance of their production. These plays were supplemented by

Festival Judge and *Sunday Times* critic Harold Hobson

backstage visits, non-competing extracts from Macbeth, and a professionally-chaired, post-production forum after each competing performance. There were also talks by such notables as actor Paul Rogers, playwright John Whiting, and George Devine, the director and midwife of Look Back in Anger, which later that year was to alter irrevocably the course of British theatre.

The Sunday Times drama critic Harold Hobson was the sole judge and gave his verdict on the final day, preceded by the first of his enthralling 'whowonit?' summaries of the Festival, littered with false clues expertly calculated to make this session the most dramatic performance of the Festival. When he announced that Regent Street Polytechnic had won, there was a brief outburst of booing from some of the victorious company, who thought that Leeds University's production of Pirandello's Tonight We Improvise should have won.

People sometimes credit Clive Wolfe with founding the Festival, but that accolade is shared by The Sunday Times arts columnist and the Festival's first artistic director Kenneth Pearson, Harold Hobson, and the then NUS president Frank Copplestone: all three now sadly departed, as is Sunday Times Editor, H V Hodgson, who also supported the venture from the first.

I was merely one of the large cast of Thornton Wilder's *Our Town*, which Harold Hobson adjudged the 'best' of the four full-length finalists performed at the inaugural NUS Drama Festival; a decision which I and others unashamedly booed for its injustice to what in our minds was the clear winner: Anne Levey's brilliant production of *Tonight We Improvise*. That verdict revealed to me the fallibility and danger of artistic criticism and ensured that, when I inherited the unenviable job of following Kenneth's excellent 15 years of artistic direction, we dispensed with attempts to compare chalk with cheese, abolished every category where practicable and always asked our three professional judges to make an award for every single aspect of productions that they thought outstanding.

Clive Wolfe

1957, LONDON

The Festival in its second year moved away from Britain's only drama department, and it was London that provided the next stop for the Festival. Despite the competing attractions of the West End, it worked well enough. Whereas Bristol had the daunting Victoria Rooms, the Bristol Old Vic Theatre School, and the only purpose-built drama studio in a UK university or other seat of higher education, London offered the King George's Theatre in St Pancras Town Hall and the then adequate theatre in ULU, the University Union building. Although this second Festival expanded to nearly six days, there were only three competing plays. NUS President Roland Freeman noted a year later in his introduction to the 1958 Festival programme: 'the [1957] Festival attracted special attention by its presentation of the first London performance of Ugo Betti's Investigation. This was an excellent example of the true purpose of the Festival: to encourage student enterprise in the world of drama. Not only was the production by Bristol University students, but the play itself was translated into English by a Bristol student.'

J W James wrote in his translator's notes: 'Investigation is a work of Betti's later period. It was first produced in Milan in 1947. On that occasion the Italian critics described the play as "a work of great and admirable importance, a cry of man's horror at the evil which is within man". The outward form of the play is wholly naturalistic, but the supra-natural values introduced make the play a statement of Betti's deep concern and pity for men. It reflects his preoccupation with, and ideas on, the themes of human will and responsibility.' James went on to note that the play had been specially translated for this production by kind permission of the Betti Estate and that the translation was intended to be entirely faithful to the original, but a number of minor omissions had been made by request of the Lord Chamberlain.

Also featured at the Festival was The Maker of Dreams, a one-act fantasy by Oliphant Down. The author wrote four 'fantasies' at about the age of 21, and died fighting in France in the First World War four years later. The Maker of

A rare production photograph of 1957 Trophy-winner *Tiger at the Gates* featuring future NUS President Bill Savage

Dreams was first produced by the Scottish Repertory Theatre Company at the Royalty Theatre, Glasgow in 1921. Already the Festival was proving adept at discovering long-lost or rare work and bringing it to a wider audience.

These performances were supplemented by guest productions from RADA, Acton Technical College, University College London, and an outstandingly fine Home of the Brave, by Arthur Laurents, presented by the ad hoc American Student Drama Group. That production was not eligible to compete, which was lucky for them because it had so thrilled Harold Hobson – and everyone else – that, by way of compensation and recognition, he gave them his 'most valuable possession', the original manuscript of Waiting For Godot.

Robert Robinson chaired one of the post-show discussions, while further fine speakers included Sam Wanamaker on the first of several visits to the Festival. There was disappointment at Peter Ustinov's unavoidable absence, but Robert Morley was a more than adequate replacement.

1958, BRISTOL

Harold Hobson closed his programme essay in 1958 recalling the words of Diaghilev, upon meeting Cocteau for the first time; 'Etonnez-moi.' This was to prove prophetic.

The Bristol Evening World in May 1957 gave the first hint of what was to come at the third Festival. Under the headline 'This Young Author Scores a Hit' their correspondent wrote: 'One can never be sure about these private University productions – quality varies so much. Last night the climb up Park Street was rewarded. I'm so glad I didn't miss this production. Henry Woolf, whose work as a character actor has caught our eye before, here introduces himself as an intelligent and sensitive producer. He introduces too, an old school friend of his, Harold Pinter, who as a writer, should go on writing.'

The Bristol Evening World was not the only witness to this production of The Room; a selector from the Festival was also in attendance and the play was subsequently invited to appear at the Festival. Being a one-act play and as such not eligible for the Sunday Times Trophy, the production was included as a guest, becoming the first Festival production to be given a second showing during the event itself. Harold Hobson, always a stout and, whenever possible, controversial champion of his beliefs ('If you think you've made a mistake, say it again – louder.') happened to see The Room and was deeply impressed, as his review in The Sunday Times from January 1958 made clear.

> The Room by Harold Pinter was presented by the Old Vic Theatre School and the Department of Drama of the University. It was a revelation and the directors of the London Arts Theatre and of the English Stage Company should be after Mr Pinter before they eat their lunch today. It is a brief excursion, in a slum room, into the nightmare world of insecurity and uncertainty. It has touches of Ionesco and echoes of Beckett; and somewhere not far distant is the disturbing ghost of that Henry James who turned the screw. What exactly the plot is, where the elusive landlord really lived, who are the unexplained couple seeking lodgings, why the lorry-driver husband is so long mute, what is the parentage of the woman who clings so desperately to shabby respectability, are questions that do not admit of precise solutions. They do not need to. The play makes one stir uneasily in one's shoes, and doubt, for a moment, the comforting solidity of the earth. Duncan Ross directs it with the unstoppable speed of an Olympic runner, and students of the Old Vic School act it memorably, especially Susan Engel as the wife and Neville Gaha as the husband who suddenly leaps into a Niagara of brutal and sadistic rhetoric. Michael Ackland's set is excellent in itself as an exercise in realism, but does it fit the indeterminate and shifting boundaries of the play? No matter; The Room is an experience. I believe it was discovered, directly or indirectly, by the department of Drama. It is a matter for them of pride.
>
> The Sunday Times, January 1958

Having championed The Room so whole-heartedly at the Festival, Hobson's now famously vindicated and prophetic review of The Birthday Party, which he wrote later that year, is given a new dimension.

> Now I am well aware that Mr Pinter's play received extremely bad notices last Tuesday morning. At the moment I write these lines it is uncertain even whether the play will still be in the bill by the time they appear, though it is probable it will be seen elsewhere. Deliberately, I am willing to risk whatever reputation I have as a judge of plays by saying that The Birthday Party is not a Fourth, not even a Second, but a First; and that Mr Pinter, on the evidence of this work, possesses the most original, disturbing and arresting talent in theatrical London. I am anxious, for the simple reason that the discovery and encouragement of new dramatists of quality is at present the most important task of the British theatre, to put this matter clearly and emphatically. (…) The whole play has the same atmosphere of delicious, impalpable and hair-raising terror which makes The Turn of the Screw one of the best stories in the world. (…) Mr Pinter and The Birthday Party despite their experiences last week will be heard of again. Make a note of their names.
>
> The Sunday Times, April 1958

On the same day that Hobson got hooked on Pinter, the Festival also saw the first English production of The Shepherd's Chameleon by Eugène Ionesco, the French absurdist writer who at the time was all but unknown in Britain. The production, staged by the Dramatic Society of New College, Oxford, included in its cast one Dennis Potter.

It is nothing short of remarkable, that on one day, in only its third year, the National Student Drama Festival saw three little- or not-at-all-known playwrights, all destined to become tremendously influential, given important, possibly crucial, recognition from an event that was already, despite the preponderance of established plays, clearly at the cutting edge of British – even world – theatre.

Another prominent dramatist, Christopher Fry, a production of whose A Sleep of Prisoners went on to win the Sunday Times Trophy, was one of the distinguished speakers. Hobson later recalls the post-show discussion of the play: 'I remember 1958, not without alarm, as the Robert Robinson Festival. Nothing in any of these festivals has ever astonished me so much as Robinson's onslaught on that occasion on Christopher Fry's A Sleep of Prisoners. He called what he said that gloomy winter afternoon "An introduction to a discussion of Christopher Fry". It seemed to me more like a preliminary to a murder. Mr Robinson ripped into Fry with a moral fervour which I myself usually reserve for pointing out the defects of Sheffield United.'

Hobson (a dedicated Sheffield Wednesday man) goes on to say that it was also during this attack that he realised that Beckett and Osborne had not only arrived, but had overturned the 'poetic renaissance' embodied, in this instance, by the hapless Fry. At the Festival, the third writer had been added to those revolutionaries.

Faces of *Endgame*: Keele, 1966 (left, with Jack Emery) and Bedford College, London, 1978.

1959, LONDON

The plays competing at this year's Festival are Crime Passionnel, Six Characters in Search of an Author, He Who Gets Slapped, and The Good Woman of Szechwan. It is a formidable list and looks as though it had been put together with the deliberate intention of refuting the popular notion – to be found in colleges as well as cathedrals – that people connected in any way with the theatre are a frivolous lot. If the programme had been compiled with this motive – and of course it hasn't – it would have been compiled for entirely the wrong reason.

Harold Hobson

Hobson went on to consider teasingly what the 'right' reason for choosing a play to perform might be, before claiming to have forgotten it himself, hoping that he would be reminded before being called upon to give the prize. In the course of his musings, he made an interesting point about the collection of productions selected as finalists for the Sunday Times Drama Trophy: 'The titles give no clue at all. Nor do the authors. The plays have one, or rather two, things in common. They are all from the non-commercial, the highbrow, the avant-garde theatre. That is their first characteristic. The second is that all four belong to the avant-garde of yesterday. No Beckett, no Arden, no Pinter, no Adamov here.'

This programme note, perceptive though it is, also serves to illustrate the restrictive nature of those early festivals' concentration on the single prize. Had Hobson been running his eye down the list of non-competitors he may have felt less uneasy. On 31 December, following the afternoon's performance by the Academic Theatre of Belgrade University of Aleksandar Obrenovic's Variations, the first of many foreign language productions to visit the Festival, was a performance by the Nigerian Drama Group of a new play by the then unknown writer, now Nobel Laureate, Wole Soyinka. The following day saw the Dramatic Society of Oriel College, Oxford present Downstairs, the first play by Caryl Churchill, at 4pm. Forty-five minutes later there was a modern stage version of the Crucifixion play from the York Corpus Christi Cycle by one

Michael Kustow. This last is described in the programme by its author/adaptor thus:

The York and Townley pageants on the subject of the Crucifixion make a direct assault on the feelings of the audience. The York pageant is attributed to an unknown playwright of extraordinary talent who, for want of a better name, is usually called the 'York realist'. His flair for realistic presentation of the physically horrible is nowhere more in evidence than in this pageant, where the business of the Crucifixion is mercilessly drawn out 'until this performance of a heavy manual job by a set of rough workmen becomes a Bosch-like nightmare' (McNein p.622).

Within two days the Festival was presenting three plays by students, all of whom were challenging the reliance on the old avant-garde. However, it was the evergreen Six Characters in Search of an Author from Birmingham University, with Geoffrey Hutchings and Rosemary Kernan outstanding, to which Hobson awarded the Sunday Times Trophy, despite competition from Leeds, Hull and Bangor.

1960, OXFORD

> The Annual Drama Festival has now become a firmly established event and includes more plays than ever before – a mammoth programme, offering unlimited opportunities for student drama enthusiasts to discuss, criticise, comment and enjoy.
>
> Dennis Grennan, NUS President

The first Festival of the 1960s ideally demonstrated the range of drama being produced at that time by students. There were four heavyweight, classical plays including Hamlet (well played by Tony Garnett), an excellent The Duchess of Malfi with Terry Hands, Geoffrey Hutchings and Peter James in the cast, a production of Coriolanus and a rare performance of The Beauty from Samos, an early play by Menander, described in a programme note as 'an innovation in Greek theatre and as such the beginning of farcical comedy'. It was translated from Charles Cordier's French version by Sheffield students Joanna Richardson and Patric Dickenson into 'idiomatic English, making the play remarkable for its modernity'.

These were presented alongside five avant-garde, absurdist plays by Ghelderode, N F Simpson, Arrabal and two by Ionesco, as well as productions of the contemporary dramas The Sport of My Mad Mother and The Kitchen. The latter play's author Arnold Wesker was one of the distinguished speakers, as was Ralph Richardson.

The Festival also featured a Polish student group from Gdansk performing The Circus Tralabomba, which Kenneth Pearson introduces in the programme: 'Its satirical voice is both loud and sharp. The Circus Tralabomba comments on life through the age-old image of the sawdust ring. It is particularly suited to production before English audiences, depending as it does on a great deal of mime and music.'

This added another dimension to an exceptionally satisfying Festival, which Harold Hobson later described as the first where he felt all the plays in the final were well worth seeing.

Petronella Pulsford in Oxford University's Experimental Theatre Club production of *Jenousia*, 1967

CHAPTER TWO
CLIVE WOLFE

1960
1969

In a way the National Student Drama Festival changed my life. The year was 1960. And, in my second year at Oxford, I couldn't decide what career to pursue: I wasn't sure whether I wanted to be a director or a critic. Anyway when a production I did of *The Bald Prima Donna* won an Oxford competition known as Cuppers and was recommended by Daphne Levens for the NSDF, I thought that was it: I was going to be a director.

When we first did the Ionesco before a Saturday-night Oxford audience, themselves in their cups, people fell off their chairs laughing. But something strange happened when we did the production at the Festival which that year also took place in Oxford. We played it on a Tuesday afternoon in the chill atmosphere of the Clarendon Press Institute. The same production, the same cast, the same text. Yet it barely raised a titter and sank like a lead balloon. The fault was entirely mine. I had barely re-rehearsed the show and, with the arrogance of youth, assumed all we needed to do was turn up. I had failed to realise that you need to take account of a new space and that, to achieve Ionesco's surreal ordinariness, requires the most minute attention to detail and to nuances of timing.

Harold Hobson was rightly dismissive of the show in his Saturday-morning round-up of the Festival in the Playhouse. But that did not matter. What really hit me was Hobson's own masterly sense of drama. In 1960 there were two strong contenders for the main Festival prize: as I recall, they were productions of *The Duchess of Malfi* and Ann Jellicoe's *The Sport of My Mad Mother*. Hobson praised both highly but gave the impression that the Webster was the stronger contender. Then, at the last minute, he pulled a rabbit out of the hat and gave the prize to the Jellicoe on the grounds that an adventurous experiment took precedence over a familiar classic.

Attending the Festival in later years, as a journalist, I realised that Hobson often used this device. But what really impressed me in 1960 was his eloquence, irony and wit as well as his climactic *coup de theatre*. I had, of course, been reading Hobson (and Tynan) for years. But it was hearing him on that Saturday morning in Oxford that convinced me that criticism was an occupation that required its own sense of drama as well as of natural justice. Once I became a critic myself in 1965, Harold proved a staunch ally, mentor and friend. But I wish now that I had told him how radically he changed my life in 1960 by demonstrating the panache and flair that criticism, in an ideal world, requires.

Michael Billington

1961, LEEDS

This is the first occasion on which the National Union of Students-Sunday Times Festival has dared to move out of the soft protection of the south into the bleak and bracing north. After Bristol, Oxford and London, all of them pampered cities; we have this year to face Leeds, a fortress of commerce with no nonsense about it.

The University of Leeds, and the people connected with it, have made a continuous impression on the Festival in the past. It is always a matter of some excitement to wait for the first appearance of Frederick May [head of the Italian department at Leeds University] at each Festival, to see whether he is wearing a beard or not and to find if his devotion to Pirandello still shines undimmed. And of course it always does. It is one of the few certain things in a treacherous world. Another is that if a Leeds company enters for the Sunday Times Trophy it will give a performance of technical perfection.

Harold Hobson

May's first appearance at the Festival (sans beard, in the accompanying photograph) was in the programme, with a prescient attack on the dangers of complacency:

> It's a very lively thing now, this drama Festival of ours, but I can't help wondering what sort of liveliness is implied by the preliminary entry of four productions of Serjeant Musgrave's Dance. It is well known that Harold Hobson has John Arden on his conscience. Is a large swathe of our student drama societies equally guilt-laden? Or is the experimentalism of university groups narrow and conservative?
>
> I don't think that student drama groups are more than superficially adventurous. I don't think they read enough plays. The last half-decade of revolution in the English Theatre has been a godsend to our groups, for they've been enabled to find impeccable stuff in the right language. They'll have to watch out, for they may be creating a new orthodoxy, an establishment of the unestablished – where all the rich 'four-letter' words will replace the horse brasses and copper-kettles as comfort stations of the mindless. It's wrong to mask inertia with Wesker and Pinter.

The NSDF has been, since its inception, a major event. It is now an institution, a vital one – a Festival in name and purpose, a crystallisation of always shifting forces in modern theatre.

In this 'celebrity' and fame-for-a-night era, the Festival genuinely nourishes and empowers real passion, energy, talent. And not through any misplaced indulgence. The nourishment is enriched by the creative interaction between the student performance and the commitment of seasoned professionals who give of themselves to observe participate and, yes, judge. This 'judgement' is crucial – it can be harsh, but always creative. From my own period as a student, 1959–62, I remember Harold Pinter's exhortation properly to observe a text and its rhythms he had found lacking in a production of his play *The Birthday Party*. And I remember, and mention it with pride, the favourable reaction of John Arden and Lindsay Anderson to a production I was lucky enough to be in of *Serjeant Musgrave's Dance*.

This ongoing and fruitful relationship between those already out in the 'business' and the student body ensures, each year, a true celebration of the good, the sometimes not-so-good, and even the honourable disaster – which is theatre, which is life.

May it always flourish – I personally owe it much.

Ronald Pickup

This robust attack on student complacency demonstrated an early incarnation of one of the Festival's great strengths: a readiness to provoke and challenge the Festival-goers. Sunday Times Deputy Dramatic Critic and Deputy Literary Editor J W Lambert, one of the Festival's initial organisers, offered, by contrast, a glimpse of how it felt to be living through the changes that had been sweeping through British Theatre since the Festival began:

> The theatre today, threatened on every hand, seems to me none the less to offer more actual and potential excitement, more possibilities as a medium, than at any other moment since the beginning of the 17th century. When I compare the climate of theatrical enterprise today with that prevailing when, more than 25 years ago, I began serious and concentrated play-going, I could weep for envy. I despair of conveying, to anybody under 25, the contrasting exhilaration of the last ten years, the gradual acceleration of lively new blend of emotion (with or without political and social commitment) and adventurous stagecraft, which

Liverpool University Dramatic Society had first entered the Festival arena in 1960 but failed to pass the first stage. Then in 1961 our production of *Waiting For Godot* was selected so, with a mix of excitement and trepidation, we travelled to Leeds. This proved a steep learning curve. We did well enough but came nowhere in the final reckoning. However, it was invigorating and informative to watch other productions; listen to guest speakers – what a dynamic talk by Peter O'Toole; attend workshops and nerve-wracking post-production discussions! I remember being totally gob-smacked when one student complimented us on 'the most brilliant theatrical touch in the Festival'. We waited – agog. Seemingly, during the first act of *Godot* he noticed 12 silver leaves on our tree whilst in the second act – only 11. This he earnestly informed us represented Judas' betrayal. How to respond? Smile and say nothing – in fact, one leaf had simply fallen off. Ah, but how everyone lapped up such a subtle moment of theatrical symbolism.

Martin Jenkins

continues to excite the near-senile responses of a man in his forties.

Part of the rationale behind the Festival was to facilitate knowledge of, and comparisons between, the hitherto isolated and virtually inaccessible islands of student drama activity across the country. There could hardly be a clearer illustration of the variety in contemporary British student drama than a comparison between 1960 in Oxford and 1961 in Leeds. While Oxford had a programme composed only of extant texts, for Leeds, four new, student-written plays were included, compared to none the previous year.

Ironically, given the speculation in the Festival's programme, it was indeed the technically perfect production of Serjeant Musgrave's Dance from Leeds University, starring Ronald Pickup, that collected the Sunday Times Trophy. A new prize for One-Act Plays, the NUS Drama Plaque, was at last introduced, and won by St Catherine's College, Cambridge, with their production of Albee's The Zoo Story.

1961 was the year the Festival received its first television coverage, with Granada Television broadcasting three ten-minute extracts from selected productions including Forbes Bramble's The Dice, a new play set in a prison cell of a totalitarian state, featuring Frank Barrie and, as Third Prisoner, one Clive Wolfe. John Whiting's A Penny for a Song, and the Sunday Times Trophy-winning Serjeant Musgrave's Dance also appeared, interspersed with comments from the Festival's artistic director Kenneth Pearson.

1962, BRISTOL

So, for a second time, we are returning to Bristol, the place where it all started.

Harold Hobson

In an essay in the Festival's programme, J W Lambert offered a thoughtful critique of the plays which were being presented by students for selection;

Of the 42 plays on the list, four were new, unpublished, perhaps specially written for the groups which presented them. Of the rest, more than three quarters were plays, not merely of this century but of our own era. There was only one Shakespeare, one Marlowe and one boldly antiquarian shot at Tourneur.

With Pinter the case is very different. With five productions of his plays in the list, he had a clear lead over all other contemporary dramatists, and as far as the universities are concerned must clearly be acclaimed 'playwright of the year' – on the strength of two productions of The Dumb Waiter and three of The Birthday Party.

The preference for Pinter seems to me significant, for despite his use of common speech he is anything but a naturalistic writer; he is a fantasist – and this I think is what has given him the lead. Pinter has a vogue, perhaps, but only because he supplies something deeply needed.

In the intervening years between The Room's appearance at the Bristol Festival of 1958 and the beginning of 1962, Harold Pinter had become an enormous success. Later that year A Night Out was seen by an audience of 6.4 million, a record for a single television drama, and three days later his play The Caretaker would open to near universal acclaim. Of the entered productions, one each of The Dumb Waiter and The Birthday Party had been selected to perform at the Festival, while Pinter himself gave a rare talk on being a writer, now published as the introduction to the first volume of his collected plays. Pinter also attended the post-show discussions. Martin Jenkins remembers one electric confrontation when an abrasive voice enquired why the director of The Birthday Party had taken liberties with the author's precise instructions. The director gave a very lengthy, somewhat arrogant explanation, only to be roundly upbraided by a stern, and until then unnoticed, Harold Pinter.

Pirandello's *Henry IV*, Liverpool University, 1962

The Festival's international reach widened with visiting companies from Madrid University and the Moscow Theatre Institute Company, as well as British universities' performances of Ernst Toller's Draw the Fires – an expressionist play of a German naval mutiny, Buchner's Woyzeck ('produced', that is, directed, by future Film Censor Robin Duval), Pirandello's Henry IV (Martin Jenkins lead actor and director again), an Ionesco and a Ghelderode. University College Aberystwyth won the first award for Wales in four years: the NUS Plaque, for the premiere of The View From Poppa's Head, by Gwyn Williams.

Actors who appeared at the Festival included: Tessa (later Baroness) Blackstone; Bruce Myers, who became a Peter Brook regular; Ronald Pickup again; Joanna van Gyseghem; Janet Dale; Alan Dossor, who would become the Greenwich Theatre Director and, acting in Bristol University's Trophy-winning Camino Real, Glen Walford, a future NSDF selector, judge, workshop director and Trustee, and founder of the London Bubble Theatre. Glen, like Alan Dossor, was later to become Director of the Liverpool Everyman Theatre, which itself owed its genesis to the 1961 Festival meeting of Terry Hands, Peter James and Martin Jenkins and support from The Sunday Times.

'And the Award goes to Bristol.' We sat in stunned silence. It was the bleak, bitter winter of 1962; the venue, Bristol. Having battled through blizzards and snowdrifts, we had overcome raging temperatures and hacking coughs to present Pirandello's *Henry IV* to a highly enthusiastic audience (lots of stamping and cheering). Things looked good. Then came the final adjudication by the veteran *Sunday Times* theatre critic, Harold Hobson. He too heaped praise on our efforts (still good) but then, right at the end, announced he was giving the major award to Bristol. There was an audible gasp in the auditorium, so convinced were most people that Liverpool had won, but they had reckoned without Hobson. His brilliant, often controversial adjudications were the undoubted highlight of each Festival – a *tour de force* always finishing, as in any good thriller, with an unexpected twist – and in 1962, we were that twist.

Martin Jenkins

1963, LOUGHBOROUGH

Loughborough, in the snow, was decidedly cold for the 1963 event, particularly for the University of Cape Town Little Theatre with guest production *The Sport of My Mad Mother*. They would be welcomed back in 1995 to celebrate the end of the Apartheid regime.

The number of cast members destined to become successful professionals was smaller than usual, but included, in the first of his three Festivals for Southampton University, John Nettles. Making his triumphant last of three appearances for Liverpool University, as lead actor and director, Martin Jenkins stormed his way to the Sunday Times Trophy with Ibsen's *Brand*.

Liverpool featured in three consecutive Festivals culminating in our production of *Brand* in 1963 when we won the Best Production and Best Actor awards. By this time, I was acting with the RSC but also working with amongst others Peter James and Terry Hands (both Festival participants) on establishing a young company which would produce plays for young audiences. Most importantly, the Festivals of 1961/2 had provided the creative springboard for arguably the most influential regional theatre of the past forty years – the Liverpool Everyman.

Martin Jenkins

Also at the Festival, cutting his directorial teeth before graduate triumphs with the Royal Exchange Theatre, Braham Murray from University College, Oxford made his Festival debut with one of two plays by Ionesco at the Festival: The Lesson.

Other notable student participants were future professional actors Ralph Bates and Margaret Ollerenshaw, and the future play publisher Nick Hern.

1963 was also the year that the Festival took its first tentative step towards the addition of journalism to the range of opportunities it offered. The News Sheet was reborn as the magazine *Noises Off*, carrying reviews of shows, discussion pieces and comment, occupying several students for several hours overnight. At this stage, it was nothing like the formidable operation of its successors from the 1970s onward, when it was to develop into a full-scale newsmag of ever increasing page and word counts, with daily issues produced through the night by a dedicated handful of students, some graduate help and contributions from anyone at the Festival who wanted to write, staple, or make coffee.

The members of Liverpool University Dramatic Society with the *Sunday Times* Trophy won by their 1963 production of *Brand*.

1964, ABERYSTWYTH

An early production of Ionesco's *The Chairs* from 1964

'Is it not possible that theatre has lived too long on Waiting for Godot and Look Back in Anger and Bertolt Brecht?' asked Harold Hobson at the opening of the 1964 Festival. As if in reply, Ionesco was the flavour of the week. There were four productions of his plays; including the rarely seen, full-length play The Killer and two different productions of The Chairs, with the version from Exeter winning the NUS Plaque. An excellent production of his play Rhinoceros by University College, Oxford, directed by Braham Murray, whose company included Peter Sissons, Michael Elwyn, Michael York, and Bob (later Lord) Scott, was beaten to the Trophy by a production of Three Sisters from Leeds University featuring the late Neil Cunningham. Harold Hobson admitted many years later that his decision on that occasion might have been his only error of judgement.

Outside of the competition, an invited company from the Theatre Academy of Bratislava presented Uncle Maroje and the Others by Marin Drzic. Kenneth Pearson later remembers, 'A mirror-flat sea glued to the beach at Aberystwyth – a freak season maniacally enjoyed, especially by the customarily land-locked Czechs.' There was also a rare performance by Nottingham University, of the Noh play Kiyotsune by Zeami Motokiyo. Other events on the programme included the eminent theatre critic and National Theatre literary manager Kenneth Tynan in conversation with famed Royal Court and National Theatre director William Gaskill. John Neville paid his second visit to the Festival, Kenneth Griffith and Clifford Williams their first.

1965, SOUTHAMPTON

At the start of the tenth Festival, Harold Hobson made two proposals:

> It is the one-act plays that have widened the intellectual horizons of these festivals. I should like to see a similar daring in the other section. It would be refreshing to be offered something the West End has never thought of.

He went on to look at a number of neglected European texts, which were not available in England:

> Why do we not translate them ourselves? Bristol, for example, where the drama school is combined with study of a foreign language, could become a positive factory of English translations of professionally ignored foreign plays of value.
>
> This then is the first reform which I should like to propose for your consideration as we celebrate the tenth of our Drama Festivals. I should like to see the Festival strongly developing the practice of discovering and presenting plays that can be seen nowhere else in the country. If ever the time comes when all the full-length plays that get to the final of the Festival are productions of plays that have never before been seen in Britain, then the Festival will truly have established itself as a force in British theatre.

It is worth noting that, in the ten years since the first Festival, when the School of Drama at Bristol was the only such faculty in Britain, it had been joined by drama departments established at Manchester, Birmingham and Hull. While in 1955 two in five entries for the Festival were likely to have been Shakespeare, ten years on that ratio had already slumped to one in twenty. Hobson's second proposal was, if anything, even more radical:

> The second is in the matter of adjudication. I suggest that we put this into operation at once, beginning with this year's Festival. I would like to see the Sunday Times Trophy awarded as the result of a popular vote.

This proposition was not taken up, but Hobson did invite two more people to join him in judging the tenth Festival. It was another two years before Rona Laurie (Chairman [sic] of the Guild of Drama Adjudicators) and Clive Wolfe (then an established Festival Selector) would be acknowledged either in the programme or by full participation in Harold's judging process. Hobson continued to be the only, but still enthralling, summariser.

Coincidentally, the Festival saw three outstanding finalists from the five full-length competing plays, and each judge preferred a different one – Harold: The Crucible (Manchester); Rona: The Visit (Birmingham); Clive: Next Time I'll Sing to You (Durham). This last, a play by James Saunders, begins as a search for the meaning of the life of the Hermit of Great Canfield, who spent his last 36 years

Robert Stephens and Joan Plowright during a discussion at the 1965 Festival

It has been nigh on forty years since I appeared at the NSDF but it feels like it was this morning. It was the 1960s and we students during that radical decade were fearless. Anything and everything from Sartre to Shakespeare we attacked with that muscular enthusiasm which is the special prerogative of youth. Nothing was safe from our attentions, nothing was sacred and certainly nothing too difficult, which is, of course, as it should be. We were the young ones and young ones shouldn't be afraid and armed with that fearlessness we mounted a production of *Caligula* by Camus, the philosophical goalkeeper. Oh yes we could talk forever through the cigarette smoke and over the beer mugs about the nature of existential angst, the moral lacunae in being and the impossibility of metaphysical knowledge. We knew all about that! We knew less, considerably less, about simple stagecraft but we were undeterred.

We few, we histrionically challenged few, performed our play at Bradford and by some extraordinary chance won the good opinion of the great *Sunday Times* theatre critic, Harold Hobson and the major prize for that year. Were we pleased! As part of that prize we got to perform the play in London at the St Martin's Theatre where *The Mousetrap* now plays. We got very nice reviews in the press and so did the costumes and props that we had borrowed from the Kenneth Haigh production which had just closed in the West End. I was particularly pleased with a review that appeared in the *Guardian* read down the phone to me by my mum. It said, as I remember embarrassingly well, 'John Nettles in the title role gives a very good performance.' 'How right,' I thought. 'What a fine critic and when do I start at the RSC?'

Later it was pointed out to me, by a friendly fellow actor that my mother had been quoting from an abbreviated review that appeared in the provinces. The fuller version published in London read 'John Nettles in the title role gives a very good performance, I suppose, by student standards. It is just a pity that, as yet he lacks the technique, the stage presence and the voice to give proper expression to Camus's tortured hero.'

And that was right too. It was all to learn. Forty years on and I am still learning but it has been, still is, a hugely enjoyable career, and for all of this I thank, belatedly but sincerely, Clive Wolfe and the NSDF.

John Nettles

Poster advertising the Festival's first West End season, outside the St Martin's Theatre

unbalanced to be popular. An unruly genius and a rebel against classic form… Comedy, Satire, Irony and Deeper Meaning, published in 1827, did not improve Grabbe's position or his prospects…' The Encyclopaedia Britannica is more succinct: 'His plays were boldly experimental in form and rich in ideas, but seldom meet the practical demands of the theatre.'

Meanwhile, the Goethe University of Frankfurt offered a guest production of Plutos by Aristophanes, perhaps in an attempt to distract attention from criticism of their unfairly maligned dramatist.

The Festival also experienced its first visit by a member of the Government: Jennie Lee, who had been appointed Britain's first Minister of Arts in 1964 and had been responsible for significantly increased funding for the arts.

At the close of the Festival three productions transferred for the week-long West End season, which did no disservice to the Festival. Peter Bridge may indeed have felt amply rewarded when John Nettles's magnificently energised and playful Caligula took the audiences by storm in Southampton's production of the Camus play. Festival Judge Rona Laurie remembers:

> I vividly recall what were for me some of the highlights during the years 1965–70. One was the performance of John Nettles as Caligula in Southampton University's 1966 production. I wrote at the time, 'Here is a young actor of great promise; he has the temperament, the intellect and the voice to do well in the professional theatre.' Now, every time that I see him in the Midsomer Murders on television, I think of that early performance.

In Keele's Endgame, Jack Emery's Hamm proved to be anything but. Non-award-winner Act Without Words, performed by Geoff Hoyle from Birmingham University, completed the NSDF's first and hugely successful West End programme – one which helped some sceptics to revise their low rating of the student drama that they had never actually experienced. Peter Bridge announced a repeat of the offer for 1967, at the larger Garrick Theatre, little dreaming that a major new directorial talent would emerge.

1967, CARDIFF

With a transfer to the Garrick the huge prize now offered by the Festival, 1967, perhaps coincidentally, set a new record number of nearly a hundred applications to perform. Standards had been rising steadily and the number of students participating this year who were destined to become significant professionals is formidable: Patrick Barlow; Howard Davies (RSC & RNT director); John Dove (Hampstead Theatre director); Keith Drinkel; Geoffrey Durham (aka The Great Soprendo); Ed Thomason; Barry Kyle; Jim Hiley; Colin Jeavons; Gary Peacock; Snoo Wilson; Jeremy Treglown; Pete Postlethwaite; Alan Yentob; Timothy Knightley; Michael Wearing and Anthony Clark. There was no visiting foreign

Alan Yentob in *The Chinese Wall*, 1967

Yes. It seems like only yesterday. It was of course a lifetime ago; well, do you remember the 1960s?

The Chinese Wall was one of those shows that was ahead of its time – an agit-prop quasi-historical polemic, penned by German playwright Max Frisch, and crudely translated into English... Does that sound indigestible? Well perhaps, but it did have *ambition*. It was epic in scale, but with parts for everyone. And at its epicentre there was me – a chain-smoking, long-winded 'intellectual' railing against – well, just about everything. And all this taking place on a university campus in the North of England two years before the Paris riots of 1968. We won. Most probably undeservedly. But hey, let's not quibble.

What I recall most vividly was a wounding review from the *Sunday Times* theatre critic Harold Hobson, which momentarily dented my self-esteem. Then there was the weird experience of driving into the West End to the Garrick Theatre – minutes before the curtain went up – still struggling to find a parking place. That experience did wonders for my stress control in years to come. During the interval it was oddly comforting to wallow in the sanctuary of Margaret Leighton's A-List dressing room with floral tributes and throat lozenges in profligate supply. The downside though was a smoking habit that has taken me over twenty years (and still counting) to kick.

So, all in all, I owe the NSDF a debt of gratitude for my first full-blooded initiation into showbiz. And for better or worse I've still managed to hang in there, even though I've been relegated from front of house to back room boy – thanks to Harold Hobson!

Alan Yentob

student company this time, but the Royal Shakespeare Theatre Company fielded a strong team for two enthralling sessions.

At the end of the Festival, three productions transferred to the Garrick: Notes From Underground, adapted and directed by Buzz Goodbody; Spare, with Jim Hiley directing, and Leeds University's The Chinese Wall, featuring a young Alan Yentob as the central Contemporary. There was a sensational result of the Garrick run for Buzz Goodbody. Her brother John remembers:

> Buzz immediately attracted offers from various television companies, James Bond producer Harry Saltzman, and John Barton, then a director of the Royal Shakespeare Company, who was impressed by the originality of the production. He needed a personal assistant and employed Buzz the following year. A feminist and communist, she always insisted that productions should be politically relevant. She began directing on the fringes of the RSC, graduating to assistant director, eventually taking on Theatregoround, the section of the company which was aimed at schoolchildren.

> Her first significant production was King John in 1970, followed by As You Like It three years later on the main Stratford stage, when she became the first female to direct a play for the RSC. Buzz then took over the artistic responsibility for The Other Place, the RSC's new centre, only 300 metres from the main theatre. Here she concentrated on cutting down the original texts for the small auditorium by producing concentrated versions of well-known plays. King Lear was staged in 1974 but an even greater success was Hamlet the following year, which featured Ben Kingsley, as the Prince, and Charles Dance as Fortinbras. Buzz committed suicide in her Islington house in April 1975, the week that Hamlet began its run at Stratford. An RSC rehearsal studio and a tree commemorate her name in Stratford. At the NSDF, the annual Buzz Goodbody Student Director Award is funded by the proceeds from a Celebration of Buzz by some of her many admirers, staged at the Aldwych Theatre on 7 December 1975 and one ten years later held at Stratford featuring Dame Peggy Ashcroft and Ben Kingsley. Marcelle Goodbody later left the trust fund a generous legacy.

Leeds University's production of *The Chinese Wall* by Max Frisch

1968, BRADFORD

The 13th Festival, returning to Bradford in 1968, proved unlucky for Harold Hobson, who was indisposed and unable to attend, and for the Festival's financial outlook.

Among the distinguished speakers and discussion chairmen were the formidable Arts Council Chairman Lord Goodman, playwright Tom Stoppard, actor John Neville and unsung champion of the NSDF, J W Lambert.

There was plenty of competition for both trophies from an eclectic field that included two plays by Harold Pinter, two plays by the little known Arrabal and one each by Ionesco and Armand Gatti. There was also a range of established plays by writers as diverse as Aristophanes, Anouilh, Weiss, Beckett and Brecht as well as a new play by Exeter lecturer John Rudlin. But the remaining two judges had no doubt that the best productions were the two last performances: both Pinters and on the same final day. The Room won the NUS plaque for Brighton Students' Federation, featuring an outstanding performance from

Sarah Willis, while Edinburgh University's production of The Homecoming, which featured the future Chief Executive of Granada Television Stephen Morrison, won the Sunday Times Trophy, in spite of the Scottish Morrison's appalling 'Cockney' accent, which even Dick van Dyke in Mary Poppins would have found hard to credit.

However, in spite of continuing artistic success, the NUS's slack financial control of the Festival had finally proved too much for The Sunday Times, which announced that it intended to cease its patronage following the particularly profligate 1968 event. Fortunately, Clive Wolfe, by then a selector, judging panel member and erstwhile reluctant businessman, was able to convince The Sunday Times that their expenditure could be controlled and somewhat reduced. As a result, Clive Wolfe was asked to become the Festival's first 'professional' Administrator. The paper agreed to continue its support for the Festival for the time being, on the understanding that Clive would take over the NUS's role and develop the organisation. Kenneth

Pearson also agreed to continue as Artistic Director, but indicated that he wanted to stand down after the next Festival. As it turned out, Pearson stayed until 1970, but the jolt to the Festival's organisational structure created by his announcement was to trigger far greater problems in the next few years.

The National Student Drama Festival hung like a dream before me throughout my time as a student at Bristol University. In 1964, my first year, I gave a misguided performance in a small part in *The Devils*, a production which didn't make the cut. The next year I wasn't in the production that was considered. However, in 1966 I really thought we would make it with *The Entertainer*, in which Archie was brilliantly portrayed by Ian Gardhouse ('Nice Mr Gardhouse' as Ned Sherrin used to call him on *Loose Ends*, which Ian conceived and produced for many years). I played Billy Rice, the father. Clive Wolfe came to a company party after the show, and I had hopes, but we missed out. So…how did I make the final? Well, I cheated.

I left the Drama Department and went to the Bristol Old Vic Theatre School, and in 1967 I was asked to play Hero in Anouilh's *The Rehearsal* for my old Alma Mater. It was very well acted, costumed and staged, and we made the final in Bradford 1968. There we lost out narrowly to Edinburgh's *The Homecoming* – which boasted a young Ian Charleson, and David Rintoul! It was directed by Peter Farrago, a born impresario, who put together from the talent at Bradford, a cast which performed *Mandrake, The Musical* (by Mike Alfreds) at the next Edinburgh Festival. It included Ian, David, myself, and David Edgar as the Apothecary. Twenty years later, I played the lead in David's wonderful play *Entertaining Strangers* (directed by Peter Hall), at the National.

In *The Rehearsal* was an actor with whom I am working as I write – doing *Hecuba* at the Donmar: Nicholas Day. We also did *The Iceman Cometh* together. In our student days, Nick gave the finest Soliony I have ever seen. In Bradford, we were in the canteen together, when a young girl came in who took our breath away – Judy Loe: she played my wife, when I was *The Chief* (Anglia TV, 1989–91).

I think you get the picture. The NSDF was a seedbed. People keen on theatre met up, and wallowed in drama for five days. It was competitive. It was exciting. And it created relationships that run like threads through the fabric of our profession.

And I still think *The Entertainer* should have made it.

Tim Pigott-Smith

1969, EXETER

With HRH Prince Charles, acting in Trinity College Cambridge's entry The Erpingham Camp (by Joe Orton), failing to be selected for the Festival, it was clear from the outset that 1969 was no ordinary year. The Festival was held in Exeter's brand new Northcott Theatre and the far from new Washington Singer Laboratories and, despite a

Birmingham University's *Waiting for Godot,* 1968

newly instituted experimental rule that all the full-length plays had to be new, which understandably resulted in some weaker finalists, 1969 had quite possibly the best drama yet. There was a brilliant adaptation of Kafka's Metamorphosis by John Abulafia starring rubber-limbed Paddy Fletcher, but Gwydion Tomas, grandson of the eminent poet, in Trinity College, Cambridge's production of Krapp's Last Tape elegantly stole the NUS Plaque from a Metamorphosis which easily rivalled Berkoff's later version, due in part to Harold Hobson's family values having been offended.

A witty, devised ensemble piece RAW ('war' backwards) also raised the roof. This show, from Rolle College Exmouth, appeared to be the first example of a new genre to be seen at the Festival. There was no official provision for anything other than the two established awards, both for productions of scripted plays, and so the three judges forked out some compensatory cash for the inventive excellence of this meticulous and funny play. Less successful was Clearway, a play of impenetrable pretensions set under a huge flyover, spectacularly designed by Saul Radomsky, directed by James O'Brien, who went on to direct the award-winning adaptation of The Jewel in the Crown.

The Amazing Harold Show, effectively an authorised fringe event, proved to be a disappointment in not being about Hobson; but so exciting and stimulating were the short plays at the Festival that three of the finalists for the NUS Plaque transferred, in a ground-breaking invitation, to Oxford in the hope that they would widen the University thespians' theatrical horizons and knowledge. Meanwhile Zoo Zoo Widdershins Zoo, the first stage play by Emmerdale Farm pioneer Kevin Laffan, featuring an outstanding performance from a young Margot Leicester, was given a professional national tour.

1969 also saw the Festival's first workshops, tentatively entitled 'Acting Studies of the Previous Night's Plays'. There were five of these in all, destined to rise to over 100 in later years. The first leaders of these experimental sessions included Charles Marowitz, Robert Stephens and Terry Hands. Also for the first time, every post-show discussion was chaired by the same person, Professor Moelwyn Merchant, giving continuity to the forums. Yet another first

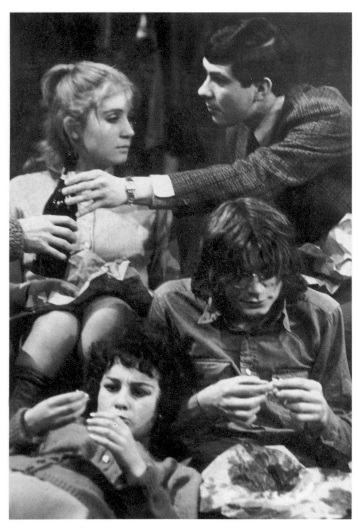

was registered when three shows, one of which had not been performed during the Festival, were staged for local audiences after the final event, the adjudication.

1969 was the last year that Harold Hobson participated in the Festival. Despite his huge physical handicaps, resulting from polio in his infancy, he had given magnificent service for all fourteen years, as judge, critic and motivator; with his idiosyncratic decisions, predilection for everything French and much admired Festival summaries. He would be sorely missed.

above: *Zoo, Zoo Widdershins Zoo* from Leicester University, 1969
right: John Abulafia's adaptation of Kafka's *Metamorphosis*, 1969

Harold was the first British theatre critic to be knighted for his service to theatre. I greatly admired him: the man's brain and writing ability, if not all of his judgements. How he overcame his tragic crippling by polio, which left him with terrible physical problems that would have wrecked theatre-going for a lesser mortal, I really cannot comprehend; nor, however, how he could be so perverse a slave to his Christian Science beliefs when judging talented students in plays imbued with contrary philosophies. Harold was at times devilish to work with; but the thousands who have benefited from the NSDF owe him a great debt of gratitude for his important part in its creation, and for helping to keep it going for 15 years. His inspirational dedication and truly outstanding service to both the Festival and world theatre are beyond reckoning. Sadly, the great little man, who famously championed Beckett and Pinter against the critical masses, has now died, predeceased by his wonderful wife/companion/nurse Elizabeth.

Clive Wolfe

top and middle: The Festival's first devised award-winner, *Raw*, 1969
bottom: Nottingham University's production of *Clearway*, 1969
right: Trinity College Cambridge's production of *Krapp's Last Tape*, 1969

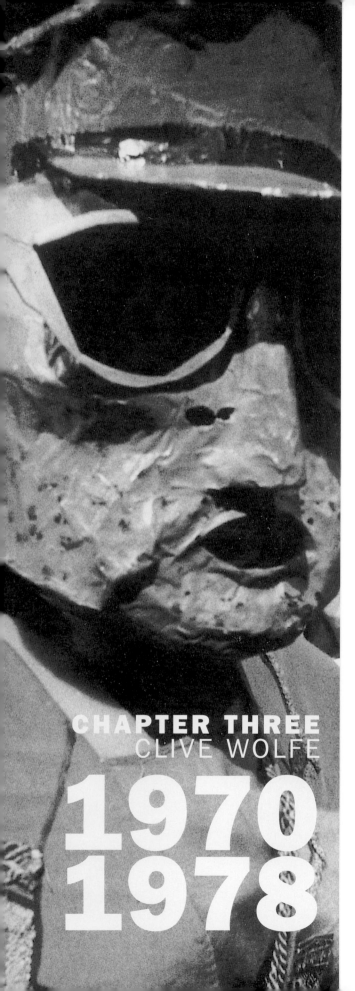

CHAPTER THREE
CLIVE WOLFE
1970
1978

1970, MANCHESTER

Gloom prevailed as the 1970 circus arrived in Manchester, to be greeted by an article in the Manchester Evening News attacking the Festival before it had even opened. Worse was to follow. The 1960s had just finished and student politics were dominated by a hard-left revolutionary tendency born in the Paris riots of 1968. On top of this militancy, BBC2 was producing a documentary of the Festival. Less heat might well have been generated without the stimulating influence of the cameras.

At one point during the Festival Laurence Olivier, unexpectedly accompanying his wife Joan Plowright who was giving a workshop, agreed to attend Birmingham's performance of Lope de Vega's Peribañez. The performers were not exactly of the calibre to which he was accustomed, but nevertheless, Sir Laurence indicated that he was not for skipping part two. However, Olivier was deliberately prevented from resuming his place after the interval by a student who had 'occupied' his seat and he watched the second half from the aisle, having refused another student's offer of a seat. Olivier also witnessed a disgraceful physical confrontation between two impressively built students and the discussion leader for this performance, the much-

York University's *Papadopoulos Rex*, 1974

respected Royal Exchange director Michael Elliot, whose calmness and dignity averted actual fisticuffs.

As all the full length plays and half the one-act plays at Exeter had been new, it was decided that everything entered for selection for the 1970 Festival had to be new to this country. This policy had a conspicuous success in the form of From Out of a Box, a short play about prejudice set in a toy-box. It was the first play by accountant George MacEwan Green and was written in response to an advert placed in The Spectator by Leicester University, who were looking for a new play to enter for the Festival. The first-rate Leicester company was once again greatly aided by another fine performance from Margot Leicester, already marked out after Zoo Zoo Widdershins Zoo for an excellent professional career. The play easily led the field to win the NUS Plaque, and was later renamed Ritual For Dolls for a subsequent professional national tour.

Elsewhere, Jeremy James Taylor made his second Festival contribution, designing and directing Durham's Madly

Madly, while Keele presented a powerful new play Viet Rock, which featured Bill Alexander, the future artistic director of Birmingham Rep, acting and Peter Sykes both acting and directing, as he was to do for the next three Festivals.

York University became the last company to be awarded the Sunday Times Trophy, not for 'best production', as hitherto, but for originality and theatrical promise. However, in a gesture echoing that of the award's first winners, the company gave the trophy back, because they believed that Keele's Viet Rock should have won. The following night the returned trophy was stolen when the car in which it had been stowed was broken into. Intriguingly, it has never re-surfaced, although its inscribed plinth has survived.

The politics, however, continued. At 3 am on the final night, NUS President Jack Straw chaired a revolutionary

Emergency General Meeting for NUS members at the Festival aimed, reasonably enough, at greater student involvement in the running of the Festival. Whilst Artistic Director Kenneth Pearson had been persuaded to stay on for one final year, 1970 was definitely his last with the Festival. It created an opportune moment for students to try to take the hitherto dictatorial power from his successor. The meeting decided that a student-elected Working Party would to be created to 'advise on the form and content of the Festival'. But the reality proved far more sinister. Like many revolutionary groups set up to overthrow an absolute power, the revolutionaries themselves turned out to be far more doctrinaire and dogmatic than their predecessors. Clive adopted a conciliatory approach to the Working Party's initial demands, but refused to agree to all the new Working Party members becoming full Selectors irrespective of their suitability, or to the selection of only newly written or adapted shows, which were also to be ideologically vetted. The lines having been drawn, battle began:

> Well, Clive, we may have been elected to advise; but we think we should do a great deal more.

1971, SOUTHAMPTON

The 1971 Festival programme was introduced by a note from NUS President Jack Straw:

> Student drama groups have always had at least a faint suspicion of student politicians; perhaps based partly on temperament, and partly upon the feeling that student drama has less fantasy than student politics. The same has been true of Sunday Times/NUS Drama Festivals. Organised efficiently, adjudged authoritatively, there never before has been – until last year – even the finest wisp of democracy about the place. For those of us who associate any conference with procedural nightmares, attending the drama Festival was a pleasure indeed. Last year, suddenly, it was all different. In about one day flat the Festival participants managed to make up for about 12 years' neglect of democracy; discussions about greater student control went on well into the small hours: interspersed with points of order, with the familiar arguments about who was or was not eligible to stand or vote, the discussions led to the establishment of the Working Party.
>
> 'Greater democracy' and 'less competitiveness' were the two cries of the Festival. A year on, it is probably worth examining how far these slogans are applicable to a drama festival. There certainly can be greater democracy in the organisation of the Festival: in deciding the administration, the venue, and the rules of entry (new works and so on).
>
> There certainly can be provision for a little less competitiveness, in the sense that there can be more prizes of an equal status, or certain categories without prizes at all. But what does not seem possible to me is that one can exclude competitiveness or authority altogether. The situation is an inherently competitive one; whether those involved simply wish to entertain, or to transmit a more profound message, an audience, of as large a size as possible, will be sought; for it is by the size and interest of the audience that the value of the production in communication terms will be judged. Individual actors, whilst they may find real intrinsic pleasure in their work, will also be seeking after the recognition of others.
>
> But the immediate communication or entertainment values of a performance are not the sole criteria upon which judgement should be based. Repeatedly, Festivals have

Bart's Hospital's new play *The Mirror and the Star*, 1971

sought after the judgement of those whom they consider to be expert, to have greater authority, and to have opinions which are more highly valued than those of others. Whilst the broad framework of the Festival may be subject to democratic procedures, it seems to me that the narrow area of adjudication cannot be; nor should it be, unless this valuable area of judgement (additional to audience reaction) is to be lost.

Jack Straw

This reasonable tone belied the number of demands which had been made by the Working Party: only original or originally-directed works were to be included; there was to be no competition other than the selection procedure necessary to reduce entries to a manageable number (although cash awards for new writing were acceptable); slots for self-selected productions were to be provided; low-key summing-up would replace the previous, openly critical, final adjudications; the selectors were to be chosen by the Working Party; and professional fringe groups would be included in the Festival's programme.

Fortunately, the consequent reduction in presentational standards from some of the student groups that this policy entailed was made less obtrusive by the fringe groups, which proved the outstanding feature of the early part of the Festival, with performances of Pip Simmons's electrifying Superman and Albert Hunt's John Ford's Cuban Missile Crisis – a devised piece created out of material from John Ford films, accounts of the crisis, and Che Guevara's diaries.

The Welfare State organised a New Year's Eve entertainment, while Naftali Yavin's The Other Company performed Handke's Offending the Audience. The anarchic atmosphere of this show, where the audience is harangued from the stage, provoked an impressive retaliation on the part of the students: one of the audience in the theatre circle jumped down into the shocked stalls, where he was expertly caught by accomplices. To their credit, the company kept going – although somewhat shaken.

The insistence on new work also provided the Festival with some successes. Shining among the rather less inspiring student shows was the immensely well-received full-length first entry from St Bartholomew's Hospital Medical College: Paul Swain's Albion Productions Playwriting Award-winner The Mirror and the Star, based on a psychoanalysis of Nijinsky by Freud. Ironically it was as traditional a piece of theatre (complete with good acting) as had been seen for years, even including an ornate stage-within-a-stage complete with false proscenium arch. It remains a source of constant amusement to Festival director Clive Wolfe that, in the midst of voting for greater degrees of experiment and political engagement, the attending students acknowledged the show as one of the biggest hits of the Festival. Another hit was a highly energised and skilful version of The Who's Tommy, adapted and directed by future Arts Council Secretary General Graham Devlin, with Charles Sturridge, later award-winning director of Brideshead Revisited, prominent in the cast.

Milton's masque Comus was given a full period production, including a quaintly amusing 'cloggies dance troupe'; RSC playwright James Robson's play The Junior Bleeders was premiered, while Edinburgh University's monologue King Herod Explains (by Conor Cruise O'Brien – lit by John Cumming, shortly to co-found Edinburgh's Pool Theatre) was also greatly admired.

The first Sunday Times Award for playwriting was given to Gabriel Josipovici for the script of Evidence of Intimacy (Sussex), although the production itself had not been selected for the Festival. The team of selectors included the future Artistic Director of the National Theatre Richard Eyre, and writer, director and actor Jack Emery. Analysis Workshops were held in the mornings with Action Workshops in the early afternoon. But there were no formal discussions of performances. Albert Hunt delivered a gentle, uncontroversial Festival summary, the last of the Festival for several years to come.

The Bacchae adaptation *Bromius! Evohe!*, 1972

1972, BRADFORD

An explosion of performances hit Bradford in 1972 with 31 productions in six days, with the basis for entry having been changed to 'new or rarely-seen' works. The new Working Party's major contribution was an attempt to have days devoted to specific themes: Community Theatre, Political Theatre, Writers, Ritual and Tribal Theatre, and Theatre Skills. The Community Theatre day was a wild success, with numerous events and productions all day. But, on the whole, this delineation proved difficult to follow, with the necessity of interpolating unrelated selected productions into the themed days. Leading alternative companies of the period, including The John Bull Puncture Repair Kit and The Welfare State, again attended the Festival, the former giving an entertaining mock-adjudication.

Almost lost in the maze of student performances was another crop of auspicious names: Antony Sher, Bernard Hill, Time Out's Theatre Editor Jane Edwardes, and Jeremy James Taylor, the founder of the National Youth Music Theatre, all performed in Macrune's Guevara, a bizarre piece about a Scottish Marxist who dies, leaving a room covered with drawings of Che Guevara, which the room's next tenant attempts to realise in a dramatised form. Barts Hospital Medical School brought one of the new student-written plays, which was entirely different from its 1971 triumph: a largely improvised version of a short story by the show's director George Blackledge. Unselected shows appearing at the Festival included James Harold Wilson Sinks the Bismarck from Bradford Art College Theatre Group, with Albert Hunt on piano.

below: Keele's Intergalactic Space Corps' *The Marshall McLuhan Foodshow*, 1972
right: *Macrune's Guevara* (featuring Bernard Hill and Antony Sher), 1972
below right: *A Christmas Naming Ceremony*, by invited company The Welfare State

1973, DURHAM

With the major players departed from the Working Party, and Peter Sykes now the Chairman, the ideological clash was clearly not going to resolve itself: the nettle had to be grasped soon, if only to improve the standards of the shows submitted for selection. The Working Party typified many of the worst aspects of student politics in the early 1970s – obsessive bureaucracy, rabid anti-authoritarianism and an obsession with procedure which made any decision taking a near-impossibility.

Durham was the venue chosen for the 1973 showdown. A General Meeting was scheduled for 'Discussion of Selection Policy for Next Festival', chaired by one of the selectors: Sean McCarthy, then General Manager of the Tyneside Theatre Company. The NUS representative immediately objected to that appointment and proposed a vote to select an NUS nominee instead. That vote was heavily defeated and so, after a lengthy debate, and with only current NUS members voting, the motion to abolish the student-elected Working Party was passed unanimously.

The rest of the 18th Festival went well, with spirits raised by the rout of the Working Party and the prospect of returning to more traditional selection criteria in sight. The main losers as a result of Working Party policy had been the student productions. For the 1973 Festival, 14 had been chosen out of 67 entries; although other shows attended the Festival as 'self-selected', 'open house' productions – another Working Party inspired initiative. Both categories contained more poor shows than usual, such as the exceptionally slow and boring production of Ted Hughes' translation of Seneca's Oedipus, or the amazingly badly-acted and directed An Off-White Comedy, which ironically included Mark Featherstone-Witty who now runs what is possibly Britain's most effective drama school, Liverpool Institute for Performing Arts (LIPA).

Mercifully, there were also some very good productions: an excellently presented and acted Fando and Lis directed by Will Tacey, York Drama lecturer Richard Drain's greatly appreciated Life in a Chocolate Factory, and After Liverpool, with playwright Nona Shepphard in the cast, directed by

Sue Wilson, who was soon afterwards to be found restoring the fortunes of the Chester Gateway Theatre. One of the week's 'Feature Performances' was David Edgar's Tedderella, an entertaining pantomime, replete with dodgy music and lots of laughs, which had been specially written to mark the day Britain joined the Common Market. There was also a single invited foreign show: In One Breath, a Polish production from Poznan, which, though well performed, proved largely obscure due to the lack of any explanation in English.

The overall standards had dropped during the civil war, but Richard Crane's society wedding comedy Decent Things might well have won the NUS Plaque, had awards not been suspended. Suspended, that is, except for playwriting awards, one of which helped to launch a very successful career in journalism. Oxford undergraduate Tina Brown was awarded the Sunday Times Playwriting Award for the script of Under the Bamboo Tree, which Clive Wolfe premiered in the third week of the Edinburgh Festival with a scratch cast of Cambridge undergraduates, who had been headhunted and rehearsed in the preceding two weeks, whilst performing with the Footlights. It went on to the Bush Theatre and attracted the attention of Sunday Times Editor Harold (now Lord) Evans, Brown's future husband.

The Liberated Zone from Bingley College of Education, 1974

1974, CARDIFF

1974's Festival took place in the midst of chaotic conditions, with serious national fuel shortages because of industrial action by the miners, unpredictable train services thanks to rail union disputes and imminent petrol rationing, due to the new phenomenon of Arabic commercial militancy. Theatrical activity, then, was a welcome relief for all, and the new Sherman Theatre complex provided a cosy hiding place for however long the heating might last out.

The removal of the Working Party from the Festival was diplomatically glossed over in the programme, although canny readers may detect a Machiavellian note of triumph in the Festival Director's introduction:

This year's Festival is the first of the series to be presented without the participation of the National Union of Students… It is entirely understandable that the NUS might prefer to relinquish activities irrelevant to its tough battles to improve the student's lot. Regrettable though this may be in a relatively civilised society, considerations of material comfort and the abolition of harmful discrimination must inevitably take precedence over recreation and culture… The Sunday Times has asked me to express its regret at the departure of its co-pioneer in this remarkable venture and its thanks for the valuable assistance given by the NUS with earlier Festivals.

As a result of selection criteria returning to that of 'dramatically effective', rather than 'ideologically sound', the standard of presentation also returned to the level enjoyed in pre-Working Party days. Competition continued to be a dirty word for many students, so again the only awards presented were for playwriting. Angie Farrow from Coventry College of Education won the Sunday Times

43

1976, EDINBURGH

So it was that after 21 years, the NSDF held its first Festival north of the border. Although Edinburgh was already known to many students from its Fringe Festival, it was entirely another matter not having 1,000 alternative shows to consider each day. Many of the venues which housed the 14 finalists were familiar to Fringe-goers – including the Grassmarket Traverse, the Young Lyceum, the Netherbow and Herriot-Watt Students' Association. The Festival ran for a record ten days.

Thanks to the IRA, the 14 finalists did not have to face competition from an excellent production of Joe Orton's Loot from Coleraine; this had attracted death threats after selection, forcing the group to withdraw their entry. A rare piece of design-led theatre, England October 30th, 1975, was presented by Central School of Art and Design. Shown in 45-minute performances from 11am to 10pm throughout one day, it was the work of 13 students who had each visited a town or city on the day of the title and presented their impressions using early forms of multimedia. Among the shows that year was also perhaps the least attractively titled play in the Festival's fifty-year history: The Play of William Cooper and Edmund Dew-Nevett, by David Selbourne (Cambridge Mummers).

Keele presented an excellently directed new black comedy – Coup d'Etat, by Paul Bream – which featured Marcus Mortimer, whose subsequent TV production career includes many classic comedies, such as Blackadder. But there was perhaps no better performance than Philip Bird's, in UEA's production of Old Times, the sole representative of the near-obligatory Pinter.

The Key from Rose Bruford College, won the Sunday Times Playwriting Award for writer and director Robert Pugh, now an established actor. The other writing prize, given by impresario Michael Codron, went to Jacek Laskowski (St Andrews) who also directed and acted in his two-handed reworking of the Pygmalion legend, Galatea.

England October 30th, 1975, Central School of Art and Design, 1976

Technical Director Ken Hall recalls an invited production after Dr Daniel Cashman of Purdu University, Fort Wayne, discovered Frank Oates, a latter-day John McVicker, studying for an Open University degree while an inmate at Wakefield gaol, who had written a play entitled A Terrible Beauty.

It took place in a black-ruled South Africa, and concerned a white South African in prison awaiting execution by the government for having murdered a black policeman. It was particularly notable for a hanging scene that used a real gallows and had the actor actually hanging by the neck in silhouette for ten seconds before the blackout.

But it was Leeds University's production of the rarely seen German Expressionist classic, Georg Kaiser's Gas, which towered over the rest, transferred to the Roundhouse, London and earned Phil Young the only non-playwriting prize on offer, the first Buzz Goodbody Award for directing, given in honour of one of the NSDF's proudest discoveries, who had died in 1975, aged only 28.

A wonderful array of gifted theatre professionals, including Joan Bakewell, Howard Brenton, Jack Emery, Martin Esslin, David Hare, Mike Leigh, Charles Marowitz and E A Whitehead, gave talks, led discussions and took workshop sessions. At one point, John Hurt threw himself into a brief post-performance discussion to illustrate a point through demonstration, and was persuaded to continue demonstrating for a good half-hour more.

The 21st NSDF might well be regarded as its coming of age. Having weathered the difficulties of the Working Party years, the Festival had emerged with a clearer sense of its purpose, and commitment to its broad-church approach to drama. Not only was most of the staged work of exceptional quality in 1976, but 7:84's performance of Yobbo Nowt at the Festival demonstrated that the high standard of the best student shows could now easily stand comparison with that of professionals.

1976 also heralded the creation of the National Student Theatre Company, which was formed after the production of an excellent new student-written script – The Death of Private Kowalski by K W Ross – failed to satisfy the Festival selectors, leaving Ross with no obvious next step. The script was given a rehearsed reading, directed by Jack Emery and cast from auditions at the Festival. It went on to become the NSTC's highly successful flagship at the 1977 Edinburgh Fringe Festival.

Leeds University's production of Georg Kaiser's *Gas*, 1976

1977, ST ANDREWS

St Andrews was the most socially successful Festival up to that point. No doubt the fact that the Festival ran its own dedicated café and bar beneath one of the performance venues, which had been granted a drinks license that allowed the serving of liquor from 11 am to 1 am by the sheriff of Fife, contributed greatly to the exceptionally congenial atmosphere. It also owed much to John Steer, Fine Art Professor and Festival Selector and to Michael Green, who introduced The Art of Coarse Acting to the Festival.

Another factor was the presence of the Festival's first professional company-in-residence – a young Shared Experience, directed by Mike Alfreds. They not only took daily practical workshops, but also presented four tales from The Arabian Nights, acting without scenery, props, make-up or any other technical aids. The excellent cast for each play was Celia Gore-Booth, Christian Burgess, Pam Ferris, Bob Goody and Raad Rawi.

Again the selected student productions matched this high standard. Unusually, demonstrating the Festival's commitment to select the productions which were most

Roger Michell's production of *Bingo*, 1977

dramatically effective, rather than programmatically tidy, the Festival saw two productions of King Lear: an inventively lit and designed Cambridge production, featuring Kate Buffrey, and a Kabuki version of the play from Leeds.

Straying further from Shakespeare's original plays, Alex Jennings played Rosencrantz in Stoppard's Rosencrantz and Guildenstern are Dead. Roger Michell directed Alan Barker in both Edward Bond's play about the last days of Shakespeare, Bingo, and in Krapp's Last Tape. Beckett also featured heavily at the Festival, as Ken Price returned to the Festival to play Hamm in Endgame, while Jayne Chard directed Judy Ilett in Middlesex Polytechnic's Happy Days.

Middlesex Polytechnic's Trent Park campus also brought an intriguing Rozewicz play: The Interrupted Act. Welsh College performed the fun new play Hold Your Horses Mussolini!, written and directed by Simon Harries.

I went from Cambridge to St Andrews in 1977. Three of my productions had been chosen but I could only take two: *Krapp's Last Tape* and *Bingo*. Both starred the brilliant Alan Barker. Eight of us slept on the floor in a very cold room in a house owned by young academics. They were vegetarians and fed their baby daughter on something horribly pink called SosMix. I snored all night and people threw shoes at me. The best bits were the workshops with Jane Howell and Mike Alfreds, and mixing it up with other students from around the country. They all seemed much, much cooler and more advanced than the Cambridge contingent, particularly those who came from colleges with drama departments. I felt we were behind the times. I had to leave a day early to get the car back to my Mum. We drove through the night. I was asleep the next day when the phone rang. 'Get back up here! You just won the Buzz Goodbody Award!'

Roger Michell

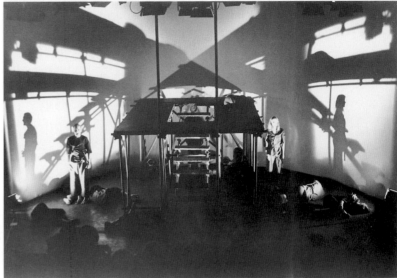

1977's two versions of *King Lear*: Leeds (left) and Cambridge (right)

Meanwhile, Stephen Jeffreys made his playwrighting debut at the Festival with Like Dolls or Angels, which featured Tim Potter, and won the hastily invented Best New Play award. Another new play was Richard Maher's Rox – given an energetic solo performance by Jon James. Phil Wharton's music accompanied Franny O'Loughlin performance as Superman in Chris Barlas' The Private Life of Superman.

In a week of impressively high standards of presentation and performance (despite two shows self-destructing), one new play, only half an hour long, was perhaps more perfectly realised than the rest. This was the NSDF's first experience of Bretton Hall – Saturday, by Dave Jacks and Richard Lewis: a brutal dissection of the lives of a drop-out and his sluttish wife, superbly acted by Christine Kavanagh and Lewis himself.

1977 saw one of the most wonderfully stimulating celebrations of student drama that could be hoped for. The selection team, which included Michael Attenborough, John Downie, Jack Emery and Nona Shepphard, was certainly vindicated in its inclusion of so many plays from the small number of entries: 22 out of 70. It was also the year that new Associate Technical Director Ken Hall along with David Elliott, who had co-ordinated the barn two years earlier year in London, formed the technical crew, which was to streamline and challenge technical standards

As an English and Theatre Studies student at Warwick University, the NSDF was the nearest thing to acting in the professional theatre that I could imagine. Driving north (in my red Vauxhall Victor with bench seat and a column gear-change) to St Andrews in 1977 and Durham in 1978 as part of A Chosen Company of impossibly optimistic actors, technicians, and the odd director, made us all feel like we might indeed change the world. It was one of the most exciting times of my student life. The thrill of performing with the best actors and directors that the universities could muster was tempered by the realization that there was a hell of a lot of competition out there. I still treasure, and smart at, the memory of being chosen as one of the four second best actors at the St. Andrews Festival! But the NSDF offered me a fantastic opportunity to play to a wider and more critical audience, and to test the belief that acting was something that I had to spend the rest of my life doing. I shall always be grateful to Clive and the NSDF for the experience they gave me.

Alex Jennings

Stephen Jeffreys' *Like Dolls or Angels*, 1977

taken into account was that at some point the luminaire store would be empty – all luminaires having been put to use in the six venues, some of them would become additional loading on the lighting grid itself. This caused a crisis when the bases of the lighting store began to lift off the floor and for some time techies could be seen hastily assembling a vast collection of stage-weights to prevent the grid crashing down onto the stage.

at future Festivals. It also included Jan Sayer (now platforms manager at Sydney Opera House), Ray Howarth, Judy Kramer, Martin Hayes, Brian House and David Leiserach (all Bradford graduates). The technical team rapidly became notorious, primarily for unhealthy diets of pre-packed pizzas and vast lakes of Guinness.

Even in the early days, the resourcefulness of the technical team was readily apparent. A potentially hazardous roof leak in the Victory Memorial Hall theatre was fixed by the judicious use of an old galvanised bucket suspended in the grid. It caught the venue co-ordinator's imagination when he overheard a punter musing upon its purpose and quick as a flash he explained that it was a new model of luminaire that he named the 'Patt 7'. Henceforth it was known by this name. (For those not of a technical bent, all Strand Electric luminaires in those days were referred to by techies by their Pattern Numbers: Patt 23 Profile Spot, Patt 264 Bifocal Spot, Patt 243 10' Fresnel, and so on.)

Ambitious venue designs included the theatre in the round erected in the Union Theatre. It boasted a cantilevered lighting grid (designed by David Elliott) counter-balanced by a luminaire store and its contents – the weight of which was calculated on an empty lighting grid and a fully stocked luminaire store. What had not been

The NSDF was really my first taste of what it meant to be a producer. We went to St Andrews in 1977 with *Rosencrantz and Guildenstern are Dead*. I was cast as Alfred because I could fit in a barrel, and I was useful backstage. (I spent a lot of time hanging out with the crew at Warwick University Arts Centre, chain-smoking and begging for tasks.) Alex Jennings led the company. We took completely for granted how luminous he was, and vaguely assumed he might have a bit of a future if he wanted to pursue acting. Looking around at the other productions curated for the NSDF was a real wake-up call. I remember gaping at the effortless glamour of people like Roger Michell, directing a brand-new winning production, and realised that choice, judgement and verve was everything, not to mention talent. I started seeing more theatre, reading more plays, particularly new ones, and began to think about the mechanics of producing. It would take years before I got a chance to have a crack at it, but I can date the NSDF as the spark point. And I still keep bumping into august members of my peer group and remember them striding confidently down wind-swept Scottish streets in afghan coats and loudly striped leg warmers.

Caro Newling

1978, DURHAM

It is little short of a miracle that NSDF '78 took place at all. The Scottish Tourist Board, who had co-sponsored the Festival for two years and, with support from the Scottish Art Council and others, saved the event from possible extinction, wanted it to return to Scotland again. However, this was on the two conditions that it would have a considerably reduced subsidy and would be located in Glasgow. Both these conditions proved to be impracticable. Clive Wolfe could still rely on The Sunday Times for £5,000, but that wouldn't go far enough and he knew by now that the NSDF would be unlikely to attract another major co-sponsor in time. So he decided to cut what were now his own likely losses, and continue trying to enhance the Festival's prestige.

Clive asked The Sunday Times if he could use their 1977/8 grant to start a National Student Theatre Company.

Alex Jennings (kneeling) in Warwick's *Entertaining Mr Sloane*, 1978

Though I'd been at the Festival the year before at St. Andrews, acting and staging the fights in Hank Williams's *King Lear*, Durham was my first and only NSDF as a director. From Cambridge, my old school friend Jeremy Monson and I brought the devised play, *The Burning of Carthage*, a virtually unscripted and entirely improvised piece about the survivors' desperate struggle in the aftermath of nuclear war. Originally staged in the tiny intimacy of the ADC Theatre, the piece lost much of its enthusiasm and intensity in the huge 1400 seat Durham University Grand Hall, where the experience was described by *Noises Off* as: '...somewhat akin to watching a movie on a very small television with the sound turned down'.

The large cast, including star-in-the-making Sandi Toksvig, struggled bravely through their one performance, only to be confronted with a largely hostile Festival discussion led by judge Braham Murray (Manchester Royal Exchange), who quotably said of my direction that 'masturbation should be done in private'. Fortunately, judge Howard Davies (RSC) saw past the derivative plots and incoherent delivery to our genuine attempt at experiment, and gave us a judge's award for 'most innovative production' – on the condition that we used the money to hire Mike Leigh to improve our improvising and devising skills. This we duly did, enriching Mike's bank account to the tune of £75 (a week's wages back then) and took a hugely re-written, closely-scripted and well-rehearsed version of *...Carthage* up to the Edinburgh Fringe that summer, to modest success and, I hope, total vindication of Howard's faith in us.

Ivor Benjamin (Hon General Secretary, Directors' Guild of Great Britain)

The plan was to take The Death Of Private Kowalski to the 1977 Edinburgh Festival. To his astonishment, they agreed. They believed that by advertising the connection between the Festival and the Company his scheme would attract more attention, and thereby possibly enough extra finance, for 1979. This new venture also gave him an opportunity to help the winner of either the International Student Playscript Competition (ISPC) or the Sunday Times Playwriting Award, both his inventions.

So all was agreed and acted upon. But then the telephone calls started, with people asking when, not if, the 1978 NSDF would be. Clive realised that halting the momentum of the event could prove fatal. He hastily booked venues in Durham and wrote to all the ITV companies, telling them that he was working that year for nothing (true), and asking for help. Help was given by Granada TV, LWT, Thames TV, IBM, Hallmark Cards, Anglia TV, Guinness, Pitman Publishing, Margaret Ramsay and even Ian McKellen, who generously donated his excellent Acting Shakespeare solo performance. Disaster was averted. The newborn NSTC presented The Death Of Private Kowalski, and two other plays, on the 1977 Edinburgh Fringe to great acclaim, and provision was made for the NSDF to continue. All the while the Arts Council of Great Britain continued to assert that it was not allowed to finance either student performances or festivals.

St Andrews had been so satisfying that it would not be easy to beat, but Durham had several highlights nonetheless – in particular a superlative Romeo and Juliet from Bucharest, performed in Romanian. This production provides one of the oddest Festival memories, from Technical Director Ken Hall:

The Assembly Rooms theatre in Durham was an ancient venue, extremely dirty with generations of dust on every ledge, and somewhat dubious with respect to safety. It hosted a visit from the Institute of Theatrical and Cinematographic Art, Bucharest, with their performance of Romeo and Juliet. Apart from the theatrical spectacle the notable fact about this company was that it was from an Iron Curtain country, and the Cold War was still in progress.

Accompanying the players were a number of dubious 'technicians'. One individual in particular introduced himself: 'I am lightning man,' which was taken to mean lighting man. He was a thickset, swarthy individual weighing some 16 stone and someone less like a lighting man couldn't be imagined. Doubts were confirmed during a focussing session. One Patt 23 had become seized on its pivot and the technician was having no luck adjusting it. Lightning man grunted, 'I do it,' promptly sprang up to the lighting suspension point and while hanging on to the bracket with one hand grabbed the hot lighted luminaire with the other and forced it with one deft movement to the desired position. Thenceforth it was believed that he was in

Sandi Toksvig (fifth from right) in Ivor Benjamin's *The Burning of Carthage*

Rik Mayall in *Sherlock Holmes's Last Case*

fact one of the secret police that were rumoured to travel with arts companies from Eastern bloc countries.

Other highlights included Tyrone Huggins in Peter Brooks' Buzz Goodbody Award-winning Abide With Me from Leeds University; Ivor Benjamin's production of The Burning Of Carthage, and a vibrant Who's Afraid of Virginia Woolf? from Middlesex Poly at Trent Park.

On top of all this was Ian McKellen's excellent Acting Shakespeare; daily Movement workshops with John Broome; Edward Bond talking on Drama, Fascism and Culture, as well as future professionals such as Alex Jennings, Rik Mayall, Adrian Edmondson and Simon Donald appearing on stage. Each of the three judges (Howard Davies, Braham Murray and Kenneth Pearson) was allocated cash in order that he could award prizes individually. And there were no poor productions. Not a bad result for a Festival that wasn't even going to take place.

As a student actress who hadn't fathomed how all the technical bits of a show worked, let alone that there might be administrative and producing functions as well, I thought I was volunteering two hours a day to the NSDF as Reception and Press Liaison. I soon found out that you cannot ration your commitment to the NSDF like that and one week and over 100 working hours later, I knew what I wanted to do when I grew up.

I remember meeting a company from Romania at the station (what an epic journey that must have been) who stunned us all with a wonderful *Romeo and Juliet*; taking in an un-neutered tom cat belonging to Ken Hall (Technical Director) because it was evicted from Hatfield College; nervously spilling a cup of tea that I was taking to Ian McKellen in the interval of his *Acting Shakespeare*; and being completely wowed by the magicians that passed as techies and being apoplectic when they got no recognition in the Awards nor mention from the judges.

But, the NSDF showed it was possible to make a contribution through numeracy, logic and application and in return experience the exhilaration, terror and deep fulfilment that come from a creative venture. That there is a need for people who are not capable of such creativity themselves, but who can build an environment in which it is easier for artists to work. And then, through the presumption that I was capable of being useful, the NSDF gave me the confidence to try.

Barbara Matthews (currently producing, consulting and training; chair of NSDF; previous highlights include Executive Directorships of Cheek by Jowl and the Royal Court)

CHAPTER FOUR
STEPHEN JEFFREYS

1979
1989

1979, SOUTHAMPTON

The notion of the NSDF as a travelling circus restlessly traversing Britain in search of one temporary home after another came to an end in 1979. The big new idea was to visit the same venue in successive years, thus carrying over the hard-won gains of year one into what would, in theory, be a smoother year two. Broadly, the plan worked: administrators and technicians who had found workable solutions on the hoof were able to deploy them again to good effect, while gaffes and glitches could be corrected after a year's reflection. This process was the beginning of the stabilisation of the NSDF: successful practices solidified into custom, and the shape of the event assumed a new coherence.

If this approach involved a loss of spontaneity in the cause of increased professionalism, then the NSDF was a child of its age. The 1979-1990 era, where eleven Festivals were held in five different locations, almost exactly spanned the premiership of Margaret Thatcher, whose increasingly intrusive presence defined the NSDF's style as well as providing much of its content. Indeed, some Festivals were dominated by events that she had set in motion: the 1982 Festival was dwarfed by the outbreak of the Falklands War; 1984 and 1985 bracketed the miners' strike; 1986, as we shall see, was all but torpedoed by the Wapping dispute.

An overview of this distinct era would place the artistic peak early on with the triumphant 1983 Festival at Bretton Hall where show after show went up like a rocket. Thereafter a siege mentality crept in: years of misguided economic cutbacks in Art and Education cramped the resources of a generation and hindered their self-expression. After the watershed 1986 Festival the decline became marked and was not to be arrested until after the move to Scarborough.

The Southampton Festival which began the new era seemed unexceptional at the time but appears, in retrospect to be full of startling pointers and portents. Two of the great comic talents of the future were on view: Ben Elton turned in an arresting performance as Schwartz in Ivan, while Stephen Fry contributed a deliciously languid characterisation in Ken Ross' satire on the Scottish National Party Tartan. Ian Cook lit an impressive production of Barrie Keefe's Gotcha from Swansea. Next year he was to return as Technical Director and, for years to come, exerted a benign influence on all things technical.

Simon Russell Beale in Guildhall's *Die Hose*, 1983

Alan Brodie, later to become an outstanding literary agent, directed and designed a witty take on Mamet's Sexual Perversity in Chicago.

But the major turning points were journalistic. It was to be the last NSDF for Bernard Levin as Sunday Times drama critic. Like Hobson, Levin kept aloof from the fray, avoiding speaking in the discussions and minimising any personal contact. But where Hobson would weigh in on the final day with his monumental closing judgement, Levin reserved his views for an elegant and witty summary in his review. His departure saw the end of the Sunday Times critic as detached observer. From now on, the holder of this position would be in the engine room, part of the management of the Festival rather than an outsider. 1979 also saw a makeover for the Festival magazine Noises Off which had appeared patchily up to this point. When the new editorial team of Mike Lawrence and Stephen Jeffreys sat down in a tiny office and bashed out a four-page stencilled edition on a pair of World War Two typewriters, they had little notion that the bijou Festmag was embarking on a 25-year unbroken streak of publication running to over 200 editions. By the end of the week, many distinctive Noises Off features were in place.

On stage there was a startlingly atmospheric production of Synge's Riders to the Sea by Patricia Curran of Leeds and an inventive take on Tolstoy's Ivan by Anthony Clark from Manchester Umbrella. Between them they shared the Buzz Goodbody award. Umbrella also provided a high-octane reading of Gogol's Marriage directed by David Leveaux, thus initiating the company's tradition of re-interpretations of classics which was to be a feature of the 1980s.

If much of 1979 was low-key, there was an unforgettable climax when Sarah Badel provided the most incandescent piece of judging in Festival history. Eschewing the role of withdrawn commentator, she slipped on a practice skirt and, in front of a packed Nuffield Theatre audience, launched into a high-voltage improvised monologue contrasting sections of classical drama – her chant of 'Oedipus, Oedipus' still chimes in the mind – with a splutter of obscenities – a distillation of what she criticised in contemporary writing. The clarity of her point – that student drama was neglecting power and nobility for introspection and smut – was, to some extent, muddied by the clamour which her event created. Some stood and cheered; others were outraged. What was beyond question was that it was the biggest performance of the week. This fact alone vindicated her intervention.

Whilst I was at university in the 1970s I was always aware of the prestige of the NSDF and dreamt of making it there. I finally did so in 1979 when I directed a production of Sexual Perversity in Chicago by David Mamet. I will never forget meeting Clive for the first time at the pub across the road from the Crown Theatre when he told us that he enjoyed the show and that Elaine C Smith would become a star. How right he was. The Festival itself was magical. Clive's great ability and enthusiasm brought together students and professionals who worked alongside each other in a great atmosphere. I remember the excitement as though it was yesterday. I saw some great productions and first became aware of John Godber, whose production of Toys of Age blew me away. A mere two years later, following another visit to the Festival but this time as an agent, John became my first proper client.

On a personal note, it was in Southampton in 1979 (in a coffee queue!) that I met Michael Imison, who was brave enough to offer me my first job; and also my (now former) wife Rosemary Squire, who now runs the Ambassador Theatre Group. I've a lot to be grateful to Clive and the NSDF for.

Alan Brodie

1980, SOUTHAMPTON

Perhaps Badel's performance made its mark, for the work on show in the following year, the 25th Festival, went some way towards making a reply to her provocation. There was a barnstorming four hour 'poor theatre' version of Great Expectations in the debating chamber from the Royal Scottish Academy of Music and Drama; a brilliant comedy cabaret act Milktrane – a harbinger of things to come – from the mercurial urban fantasist James Maw and his deadpan saxophonist Andy Hampton; a notable calling card from James Wilby as St Eusebius in Peter Barnes' Noonday Demons; and a truly original full-length play, Potter's Wheel by Shaun Prendergast.

But the immediate inclination in 1980 was to look back in amazement. Here was the NSDF in celebratory mode, congratulating itself for surviving 25 years. In the light of what was to follow, this may not seem much of a milestone, but the shared view of those who'd been around from the early days was one of disbelief – an event with such modest beginnings was now an institution. On a sunny Sunday afternoon, many alumni reappeared for drinks and a special performance of Angie Farrow's Privitus Privitorum Privit Hedge, an NSTC hit from seasons in Edinburgh and London. The most notable and welcome guest was Harold

Hobson, witty and benevolent in what was to be his farewell appearance.

The new Sunday Times drama critic, James Fenton, began his reign and tore up the rule book. Where his predecessors had kept aloof, he waded in with vigour, participating in discussions, analysing productions with the cast over tea the day after the show and creating spontaneous events such as the closing day 1983 debate on whether writers should be abolished. Arguably the finest war correspondent and the most gifted poet of his generation, Fenton gave generously of his talent and paved the way for the Robert Hewison era which was to have an even greater impact. The Festival took Fenton to its collective heart, once spontaneously awarding him, on the final evening, a pair of lilac shoes to replace his own scuffed footwear.

At ten days, beginning on a Thursday and limping on into the morning of the Sunday following, the 1980 event proved too long. But artistically and administratively, a new momentum was building.

Top: James Wilby in Noonday Demons from Durham University

Left: A scene from Shaun Prendergast's Potter's Wheel

1981, HULL

If ever there was a venue that could have been tailor made for the NSDF it must have been Hull. It had the venues, it had the requisite intimacy, it had a fascinating infrastructure of pubs and cheap restaurants. Above all it nurtured a drama department which – either through selection or training or a happy combination of both – provided a conveyor belt line of talented, wacky and committed students. Their work on stage and in the organisation of the Festival and on its peripheries was usually outstanding and never dull. For the next few years, Hull provided the shock troops of the NSDF and NSTC armies. They had impressed in 1979 with Anna-Luse by David Mowat (the era's cult writer for the discerning student) and in 1980 when Jane Prowse won the Buzz Goodbody award for her production of The Pearl. Now, in 1981, it was the turn of Rebecca Harbord in Caroline Pugh's play A Portrait of Sarah Siddons. With great presence and gestural delicacy, Harbord brought the late-18th century tragedienne back to life in a beguiling monologue. But an even bigger impact was made by another great institution of the era, Manchester University's Umbrella company. They too had left a calling card in Southampton with the characteristically bold choice of Georg Kaiser's The Raft of the Medusa (featuring the future playwright Charlotte Keatley as Little Fox). This time they took up an even more intractable challenge with the allegedly unperformable Ben Jonson play Epicoene or The Silent Woman and succeeded in making it funny and riveting. The driving force in the company in these years was Laurence Boswell, a young man not short of confidence or ideas, but he was surrounded by talented actors including Mark Sproston, George Dillon, Sara Mair-Thomas, David Phelan, Richard Dillane, Katharine Jones, Doon Mackichan and many more.

In 1981, however, both the cavaliers of Hull and the roundheads of Manchester were upstaged by the arrival of Minsthorpe High School and Community College. John Godber, a miner's son from South Yorkshire, had made a strong NSDF debut in 1979 as co-writer and co-director (with Richard Lewis) in Toys of Age. After leaving Bretton Hall, he had returned to his geographical roots as a drama teacher. The result was Cramp, a highly personal response to the suicide of a friend, presented in promenade staging. The play's hook was the sight of its author lifting over 200 lbs of weights live on stage in the gym sequences. Godber, an immense physical presence, cunningly cast an equally fine figure of a man, Andrew Livingston, in the role of his sidekick. There was an oddness to Cramp, an absolute refusal to deal in cliché combined with an absolute commitment to wrestle with tragedy which caught the imagination. It marked the beginning of a startling career for Godber as writer, director, actor and, subsequently, presiding genius of Hull Truck. More pointedly, it would be hard to imagine him flourishing quite so readily without the existence of the NSDF: a talent as unconventional as his required an unconventional access road. Further, the impact of his emergence worked both ways: if the Festival gave Godber his break, he returned the compliment, since schools, taking notice of the Minsthorpe triumphs, began to see the NSDF as a potential stage for their young talents. Over the next twenty years, the notion of the NSDF as a playground for university students would be challenged by this youthful constituency.

St Luke's College Exeter provided an inspired satire on the education system, The Sabre-Tooth Curriculum, and Tim Dodd from Wimbledon School of Art kept alive the intermittent flame of visually based performance art with his bold and imaginative Voyage Fantastique. There was not much work of this kind coming out of British universities, an absence underlined by the Studio Herman Teirlinck, a welcome visitor from Antwerp who staged the Brothers Capek's The Insect Play and gripped the audience entirely visually (the play was given in Walloon).

The most significant development of the week was the fact that all four judges (Martin Jenkins, James Fenton, Linda Maher and Bill Alexander) joined in the discussions and led talks or workshops. Although this level of participation is now taken for granted, 1982 was the first Festival in which it happened.

Above left: Manchester University's Umbrella TC production of Lope de Vega's *The Dog in the Manger*

Above right: Minsthorpe High School's production of John Godber's *Happy Jack*

Bottom: St Luke's College, Exeter's *The Sabre Toothed Curriculum*

Prior to 1968, when Clive Wolfe became the first professional organiser of the NSDF, the selection process for the Festival was somewhat haphazard. The university or college entering the Festival would notify the NUS's Vacation Work Camps Organiser of their production, and the NUS would then ask the adjudicator who lived nearest to the institution concerned to see a performance and on their recommendation, the production was either in or out of the final Festival. This meant that there were up to 16 adjudicators deciding on the final participants without much recourse to each other. Therefore the standard in some of these earlier Festivals was variable, to say the least. Clive decided that a smaller centralised team who could frequently confer would serve the Festival better. Indeed in one Festival (1969) nearly all the most successful finalists were seen first by just two people: Clive or Kenneth Pearson. (In the first two of the years that I was a selector (1982–85) there were, aside from Clive, three of us – myself (an actor and writer), Nicholas Broadhurst (a director), and Stephen Jeffreys (a writer), all of whom were working professionals, and all of whom had considerable experience as participants in both the NSDF and the NSTC. The process was simple; Clive would check the availability of one of us to see a particular production, he would then send us a copy of the script (if there was one) and we would travel to wherever the production was and adjudicate it. There were five possible judgements: this production should be selected for the Festival (1) never (2) just possibly (3) quite possibly (4) probably (5) undoubtedly. In the case of (2) and (3) this would involve a further visit from another selector (usually Clive) and on his decision the piece would either be in or out. On rare occasions a production would so bowl the selector over that a second visit was not needed, but in general, every production that made the final Festival would be seen by at least two selectors.

After all the productions had been seen, there would be a long meeting between all the selectors to determine the final list. In general, there wasn't a set number of productions that could be accepted – this would depend on many factors: the Festival venue that year, the production sites within that venue, the length and/or technical complexity of the finalists, and so on, but the final number was usually in the region of 14 to 16.

These final meetings could be quite tempestuous – usually there were three or four productions which were dubbed 'borderline' with maybe two final places at the Festival available and all of us developed considerable skills of advocacy in championing our favourites, but as we all knew each other well and trusted each other's opinions, the decisions would always be arrived at without too much rancour, with the result that the system of selection is still broadly in use for current Festivals.

Trevor Cooper

1983, BRETTON HALL

Nothing quite prepares you for the beauty of Bretton Hall. It's a standard joke among Wakefield taxi drivers, taking potential students from the railway station for their interviews, to paint a picture of the industrial grimness of the college and then watch as their passengers gaze for the first time on the exquisite silvan setting. Certainly the magic of the landscape contributed to the success of the three Festivals held there. The sense of focus attendant on the Bretton experience led to an even closer rapport than usual between participants: everyone on site was at the Festival and there was no reason to go anywhere else. Productions were chewed over for days and themes explored in detail.

Meera Syal and giant prawn in Jacqui Shapiro's *One of Us*

I do not have a good memory for details. Much to the irritation of my friends and family, I seem to have forgotten most of what happened to me at school and college. Apart from a congenital difficulty in concentrating, this may be because I had, at that time, no firm idea of a career or profession, no big plan or ambition, no real sense of who I was. What changed that (or, at least, what finally concentrated my mind) was my involvement with the NSDF.

It happened almost by chance. A group of drama students from the Guildhall decided to do some work outside their hours at college and asked the director Jenny Killick to come up with a project. She decided, almost absurdly, to put on a German Expressionist comedy, *Die Hose* by Carl Sternheim, a difficult choice, and under her leadership, it proved to be good enough for inclusion in the Festival. She won a prize for her production, we appeared subsequently at the Traverse Theatre in Edinburgh and a couple of us, as I remember, were given precious Equity cards.

But, more importantly than any prizes or indeed the success of the show was the nature of the Festival itself – a meeting of people from different backgrounds, with a wide range of techniques and vastly different ideas and ambitions. I had never experienced anything like it, nor felt so strongly that people shared with me a profound sense that live performance was important and valuable.

It was during that time that I finally decided to become a professional actor and I was encouraged to do so by the judges of the Festival and, above all, by the great Clive Wolfe, the mastermind behind the whole event. To them, and to him, I owe an enormous debt.

Simon Russell Beale

Bill Alexander, Jimmy Jewel and Susannah Yorke

At the first Bretton Festival in 1983, there was an exceptional quantity of good material to explore. Looking back after an interval of more than twenty years, it seems impossible to believe one saw all those memorable productions in the same week. It's still harder to choose the highlight. Perhaps it was the staggering debut of Simon Russell Beale as Herr Maske in Jenny Killick's brilliant production of Sternheim's Die Hose. As soon as he came on stage you were aware that this was to be an actor of extraordinary power and individuality. Bespectacled, bow-tied and bustling, he veered between deadpan respectability and manic possession by inner demons. The rest of the company held their own around him and brought this neglected play to exuberant life.

Or then again, perhaps it was Meera (then Feroza) Syal as Nishi in Jacqui Shapiro's One of Us. She came on roller-skating with a two-foot prawn clamped to the side of her head and, after, engaging us in the inanities of working in a fish theme restaurant, provided an insightful portrayal of the life of a young woman who belonged and yet didn't.

Another superb monologue which tantalisingly revealed the dark memories of a quirky character was co-written (with Michael Duke) and performed by Simon Donald in A Tenant For Edgar Mortez. Yet another significant debutant was Kay Mellor, later to become one of the key television writers of the age. Her Paul, a portrait of a mentally handicapped teenage boy and his mother, based on a true story, was well researched and moving, avoiding all the clichés of its genre. There was also an incredibly sexy production of Chicago starring Amanda Dainty and Catherine Terry.

The design highlight of the year came with Pete Jukes's production of Synge's In the Shadow of the Glen, featuring Joanna Scanlan (whose Best Actress award for her Nora Burke foreshadowed her 2004 Oscar Nomination for Girl with a Pearl Earring). This atmospheric piece was entirely lit by candles, a piece of low-tech inspiration which stood out even in an inspiring year. Tom Hare-Duke took on the mantle of Lawrence Boswell for Manchester Umbrella and gave us a scintillating Troilus And Cressida. The great music-hall and radio comedian Jimmy Jewel stopped by to comment on Comedians, the play in which he'd made his straight acting debut at the very end of his career and the judging team of Fenton, Bill Alexander and Susannah York declared themselves suitably enthralled.

All I ever wanted to do was write. The National Student Drama Festival gave me a focus...a target. Whilst at drama school, I announced, 'I'm writing a play for the Festival...who wants their smudger in *The Sunday Times*?' We entered, got selected, and a group of students from Central School of Speech and Drama headed up to Hull to perform *The Irons*. The NSDF was a real learning curve for me as a writer (and for hundreds of others as performers). Leading practitioners in theatre were trapped with the great unwashed for days. I remember they were quite kind: Bill Alexander, an RSC director, was even quite encouraging. But as encouraging as the 'leading practitioners' were, one's fellow students could be terribly damning. There was a discussion group each morning to discuss the previous evening's plays. Standing in that room, in a cold sweat, as a few hundred people told you exactly where you went wrong, hardened me up for anything A A Gill has thrown at me since. Looking back, that first Festival taught me so much. It gave me more than just the 'opportunity'. Before that Festival, I'd never re-written. I'd write something, and get a few of us to perform it. But after that Festival, I became a fanatical re-writer. I'd only have to imagine standing up in a room full of snarling would-be actors, writers, directors. That lesson has stayed with me till this day.

I also remember watching all the other plays, desperately trying to learn (or nick) something from them. Meera Syal was performing in a play, and I remember her entrance as a waitress, on roller skates, with a giant prawn on her head, which was greeted with great enthusiasm. I made a mental note: 'First five minutes of the play, get the audience on your side.' John Godber, who was teaching at the time, had taken his school play to the Festival. I talked to John in the bar about writing and teaching, and he said 'in every child there's a story'. And with that reverberating around my head, I left drama school and started teaching.

Tony Grounds

Top: Neil Henderson as Tiresias in Anaber Theatre Company from Aberystwyth's *The Odyssey*, with two of the kettles used to create a storm atmosphere visible, 1984

Bottom: Nick Phillips' studio musical *On the Outbreath*, 1984

1984, BRETTON HALL

If there was bound to be some sense of anti-climax in the following year, the second Bretton Hall Festival was still a strong one. Annabelle Apsion played Medea under Catherine Carnie's imaginative direction for Swansea while Manchester Umbrella switched to modern classics: Denise Evans and George Usill gave a high voltage Decadence and the brooding intensity of Brenton's Christie In Love was well realised by Miriam Segal, Paddy O'Kane providing an acerbic performance. Tim Supple's The Merry Wives of Windsor was the most ambitious show on view with Andy McNish impressive as Falstaff.

Two unusual instances of the NSDF selection system's flexibility were in evidence. Polly Teale, having had her play rejected by the Manchester Umbrella committee, got on her bike and ambushed a selector during the interval of another show. Impressed by the script, the selector phoned Clive Wolfe who waived normal procedures. Teale then assembled a cast and slung the play on within a week. Selected, it triumphed at the Festival, winning the Best New Play award and launching the writer/director's glittering career. Similarly brought back from the brink was Hull's Cloud Nine. A selector, who was violently ill during the Saturday selection meeting, had recovered sufficiently by the Tuesday to feel that he had failed to argue the case for the show well enough. Three days after being declared dead, the show was resurrected and won the Company Acting Award. In both instances, Clive's common sense won through. Although there were some disadvantages inherent in the NSDF's set-up – essentially a one-man operation run from a loft in Muswell Hill – there were many instances where the lightness of the administrative baggage allowed decisions to be improvised. Increasingly through the 1980s, the influence of Pat Wolfe became a factor. Calm, shrewd and supportive, she began to use her flair for casting to help create the NSTC companies. But her greatest achievement lay in being 'the power behind the throne': without her, the continuation of the Festival would have been very doubtful indeed.

Kay Mellor's *Paul*, performed by Stephen Moffitt

Minsthorpe showed they could still operate without John Godber: they were unlucky to receive no awards for Simple Game, an insightful play by Jane Thornton, which introduced two fine new performers Adele Shaw and Adrian Hood. Mick Callaghan directed. Future Evening Standard journalist Alex Renton wrote a brilliant monologue about heroin, A Twist Of Lemon with Don Reilly performing. The play was later performed at the Cottesloe.

The two outstanding shows of the year were both celebratory: defiant outbursts of the imagination against the encroaching political darkness. The Anaber Theatre Company from Aberystwyth won the BP Company Award for The Odyssey. Instead of engaging with the original's epic qualities, Anaber went for a low-key studio effect, utilising audience participation, a small choir and homely technology (a storm at sea was created by a pair of kettles). It was over to Hull for the hit of the week: On the Outbreath a studio musical written and directed by Nick Phillips with Meg McDonald, Kate Atkins, Gill Baskeyfield and Maureen Glackin. Musically brilliant, the show's jubilant hymn to female potential defined the spirit of the age.

As well as spreading joy, On the Outbreath bequeathed the gift of a major and distinctive personality to the NSDF in the shape of its writer/director Nick Phillips. Nick became, for the next decade, the beating heart of the Festival, combining magnetic personal warmth with acute

65

1987, BRETTON HALL

Accordingly the return to Bretton Hall in 1987 was anti-climactic. The vogue was for company devised work, a process which provided the week's one copper-bottomed hit: a new version of Bœowulf created by Phil Jackson and Steve Hammond. Partly the show scored through its boldness: staged out of doors at night, lit by flaming torches with Jackson himself attacking the Old English classic with manic vigour, it contrasted well with the black box studio work on offer. Some detractors saw it as a boys' show, an attempt to revive laddish values by harking back to a romanticised, club-waving, wattle and daub past: but there was so much commitment in Jackson's howling at the night that it seemed churlish not to be swept away on the tide of his energy.

Another major source of life – again focusing on exuberant maleness – was the King Alfred School's production of Tony Grounds' Holiday in the Sun. This trenchant take on loutishness provided much amusement at the time, but is now forever tinged with sadness after the death not long afterwards of Tristan Bates who, with his twin brother Ben (sons of the actor Alan) played a leading part. A third view of masculinity – just as feisty, but unreservedly gay – came from Peter Quilter's bold performance in Harvey Fierstein's Torch Songs. But the strengths of the 1987 NSDF indicated its weaknesses. The high tide of feminist theatre which had kept British theatre afloat since the start of the decade was ebbing and with the level of entries dropping and no end in sight to the Thatcherite nightmare, hopes and standards were falling. Further, the economics of the NSDF were placing increasing pressure on participating companies. The entry fee, transport, accommodation and living costs made huge

Photograph © Allan Titmuss

Philip Jackson in Leicester Polytechnic's *Beowulf*

I returned to the Festival with the King Alfred School production of *Holiday in the Sun*. Another original work, performed by 14 massively overexcited, wild, 15 year olds. They sang all the way from London to Wakefield, and then made straight for the bar. I still hear from some of those pupils, and they all talk about the Festival as the highlight of their school lives. One of our actors, Tristan Bates, sadly died a few years after the Festival, whilst on a modelling assignment in Japan. The Tristan Bates Theatre in London was named in his memory. His twin, Ben, is an actor in New York. Another cast member, Charlie Creed-Miles, is also a very successful actor, and several others pursued careers in the media. The NSDF gave them the opportunity to see just how talented they were...and to get their smudgers in *The Sunday Times*. The play was performed with great energy, and boy did we have the audience on our side after the memorable opening five minutes! At the following morning's discussion, Clive Wolfe told me that he thought I would have a successful career as a television and film writer. I thought of myself as more of a Strindberg or Chekhov. My next play was put on ITV and I've written exclusively for film and television ever since. I wonder just how many lives Clive Wolfe and the Festival have influenced?

Tony Grounds

Left: Shelly High School's *Lonesome Road*
Right: Peter Quilter in Bretton Hall's *Torch Songs*
Bellow: King Alfred School, Hampstead's production of
Tony Grounds' play *Holiday in the Sun*

calls on already strained student resources. Companies increasingly had to scratch around making deals with local businesses to finance their participation. The big picture of the NSDF's sponsorship deal with The Sunday Times was inscribed in miniature in the story of most of the shows which made it to the Festival.

Curiously, the sheer organisational verve of the NSDF tended to mask the seriousness of the crisis. All through the 1980s, the standards and consistency of the workshop programme rose. First Nick Phillips, then Iain Ormsby-Knox, wrestled successfully with the problems of how to maintain a mixture of efficiency and spontaneity in this department. As the decade went on, the range and quality of what was on offer in the (now traditional) 9.30 am – 11 am slot increased. Such stalwarts as John Wright, Terry Besson and Huw Thomas became fixtures. (No NSDF was complete until Thomas, compering on the last night the cabaret artists he had fostered during the week, stuck a recorder up each nostril and snorted his way through a piece of Baroque counterpoint.) But the High Command sensed the need for change, and that intuition was reinforced after the two Cambridge Festivals of 1988 and 1989.

1988, CAMBRIDGE

The unquestioned highlight of 1988 was Eric Prince's *Wildsea-Wildsea*, an expressionist view of loss which was as moving as it was technically daring. Prince had featured in Festivals from as early as 1971 and had consistently championed a non-naturalistic European style of theatre. *Wildsea-Wildsea* was, perhaps, his masterpiece, moving effortlessly from introspection to retrospection to action with the aid of a talented company. Elsewhere there were debuts for the fine comic duo Andy Parsons and Henry Naylor and for Marianne Elliot who directed *The Zoo Story*. Barking College of Technology scored with *for colored girls who have considered suicide / when the rainbow is enuf*; there were four shows from Bretton Hall; and a school – North Chadderton – walked away with all the acting awards for *Orphans*.

Barking College of Technology's production of *for colored girls...*

Photograph © Allan Titmuss

I arrived at the 1988 NSDF with my mates Stewart Harcourt and Mark Jones. We had collaborated on a performance art piece for Mark to perform in called *The Breakdown*. I wrote the score, in addition to playing and dismantling a piano during the show. It was one of those shows lots of people reviewed in *Noises Off*, and I even got my own Festival stalker for a few days, which was exciting.

On the final day's summing up Mark won an award for his performance, whilst John Godber told me to stick at playing the piano as I was a lousy actor. I have been conducting musicals with my back to the audience ever since and never uttered another word on stage.

Mark's brief flirtation with celebrity got the better of him, and despite promising to split the winnings (£50) with Stewart and myself, he headed up north to spend the money on tickets for Peter Brook's *Mahabharata*, leaving the pair of us to return to Hull to write our first musical – which was inspired by seeing a fantastic production at the Festival of *for colored girls...*

The main prize that year went to *Wildsea-Wildsea* by Eric Prince, which Glen Walford praised for its sparse but beautiful opening image of four suitcases on an empty stage. That, alas, is all I can remember about it – probably because it wasn't all about me.

However, the Festival was dominated by an intense censorship debate, fuelled by Bretton Hall's production of *Damage Your Children* (featuring future *League of Gentlemen* stars Mark Gatiss and Steve Pemberton). Ironically, it was at this Festival I first met Richard Thomas, who many years later asked me to be musical director for *Jerry Springer – the Opera*. I read yesterday that *The Daily Mail* was criticising the BBC's decision to broadcast a show on network television with so many expletives in it. I wish they'd seen *Damage Your Children*.

Martin Lowe

Photograph © Allan Titmuss

Photograph © Allan Titmuss

The most controversial moment came in the summing up when John Peter (taking the place of an absent Robert Hewison) launched an attack on Ruth Ben-Tovim's production of Cement for Middlesex Polytechnic. Peter, a Hungarian with first-hand experience of Stalinism, lambasted the play's politics (which offered, in his view, too rosy a view of the Russian Revolution). In effect, this was a return to the old days when the Sunday Times critic issued judgements from on high. Peter's perceptions were accurate, but the NSDF, now accustomed to the convention of judges making their opinions known in the daily discussion, was scandalised.

Top: Eric Prince's *Wildsea-Wildsea* performed by North Riding College
Left: Middlesex Polytechnic's production of Heiner Muller's *Cement*

1989, CAMBRIDGE

The second Cambridge Festival saw the playwriting debut of Tim Fountain. Now notorious for his interactive live sex shows, Fountain made a quiet start with Harold's Day, an almost actionless drama about an old man and a papier-mâché tortoise. Rumu Sen-Gupta impressed with her direction of Darkle which won the Sunday Times playwriting award for Bill Gallagher and there was an excellent Road from Bretton Hall, appearing in their eleventh successive Festival. The Thomas Sumpter School again displayed their abilities, winning the Company Acting award for Richard Cameron's The Moon's the Madonna. For many, the outstanding show was Steve Shill's The Ode to St Cecilia from Leicester Polytechnic. Like Wildsea-Wildsea, it was the kind of theatrical experience rarely available in

Leicester Polytechnic's *The Ode to Saint Cecilia*

mainstream theatre, an account, sometimes edgy, sometimes elegiac, of a group of musicians waiting for the start of a gig. Earlier in the week a company of 70 from Roade School gave an uplifting version of Godspell which symbolised the joyful emergence of secondary schools at the NSDF in this period.

The two Cambridge Festivals were good experiences – there were numerous highlights and bonuses, not the least of which were the excellence of the Local Organisation team and the emergence of Ian Shuttleworth as the next editor of Noises Off. But the NSDF has always worked best when it has been able to impose itself on a venue, when it feels like the only important event going on. Cambridge, like – in a different vein – London, is a city which seems bigger than the Festival. Further, especially in 1989, there was a profusion of venues and no generally agreed Festival centre. The Cambridge experience added weight to the view

My adrenaline habit has been sustained over these years and in many different ways. Playing the Gypsy in Bristol's *Camino Real* was an anarchic high, further fuelled by winning the trophy that year – how we crowed...vile competitive creatures that we all were. And though Festival award-giving has become more fitting for a civilised society in recent years, if you think ferocious competition is no more, try being a fly on the wall at the annual late-night poker game. Those dear friends become deeply aggressive enemies as we fight to the death for each other's cars, lovers, mortgages, graveyard plots or anything that anyone else holds dear.

I had gone missing from the Festival for a few years. I was Artistic Director of the Liverpool Everyman when the urgent telephone call from Clive Wolfe came – 'Sheila Hancock cannot be Festival Judge – can you take her place?' 'Perhaps,' says I, the juices beginning to heat up straight away; 'when is it?' 'Now' says he. 'It's Swansea. You've already missed two shows – you'll have to watch them on video.' Instead of saying, 'Hang on – I'm in a position of solemn responsibility here – I can't just abandon everyone and swan off to Swansea,' I found myself saying 'The cavalry is on its way.' Heady stuff. So heady in fact that I found myself judging for six years. Via the 'coven' – a very secret ceremony where we three judges would wage war over whether a show was genius or risible; I found more friends and later became a member of a slightly bigger but no less passionate NSDF Board.

Glen Walford

Darkle performed by the University of East Anglia

that the future lay in a semi-permanent home with cheap accommodation where each successive year refinements to all activities could be effected by an experienced team. Strongly encouraged by Eric Prince, an advance party of Clive Wolfe, Nick Phillips, Stephen Jeffreys, Steve Garrett and Bill Richards visited Scarborough. Garrett (who was to become the first recipient of the director's special award) and Richards drew up technical plans. Phillips and Jeffreys knocked out a day-by-day outline on an Amstrad 9512. Wolfe sealed the decision. The move to Scarborough was on. For the foreseeable future, the notion of the travelling Festival had been put to bed.

Photograph © Allan Titmuss

CHAPTER FIVE
IAN SHUTTLEWORTH
1990
1999

1990

In 1990 the Festival arrived in Scarborough. Crucial support came, of course, from Sir Alan Ayckbourn (as he then wasn't). His Stephen Joseph Theatre in the Round (then in its Westwood premises which preceded its current home) was the 24-hour-focus of the Festival, as a venue for performances, discussions, socialising and also as the site of Noises Off magazine, which worked through the night in what was usually the SJT's rehearsal room. As importantly, David James – director of leisure and amenities for Scarborough – was a keen advocate for NSDF in Scarborough, so that subsequent years of funding from the local council, not least the provision of the extensive Spa Centre throughout Festival week, came to be secured.

In 1990, however, the Spa was used hardly at all by the Festival. The six performance venues included spaces at what was then North Riding College (later University College Scarborough, and ending the decade as the Scarborough campus of the University of Hull, as various institutions played pass-the-parcel with this teacher-training institution), independent school Scarborough College and the town's YMCA. The latter two became notorious for almost opposite reasons. The YMCA Theatre was one of those purpose-built performance spaces designed with no idea of what actually helped performance. It rapidly became clear that the venue acted as a kiss of death to those

It was at NSDF that I first saw what theatre could do and what it could be.

I had been selected to take a suitably over-ambitious and over-elaborate *Hamlet* to the Festival. I spent the week in a very different world, discovering the simplicity of theatrical play through a series of wonderful workshops and masterclasses. What is still burnt into my memory was 90 minutes with John Wright, one of the great theatrical teachers in the world, who introduced me to the joys of mask, buffon and clown. In one hour and a half my career was started. A year later my buffon show scooped a prize in Edinburgh. The set was one four-legged table. There were only two actors and no costume changes. I had discovered that theatre must always take place in the imagination.

David Farr

Festival productions staged in it, leading one Festivalgoer to suggest tartly, 'Let's have the pyrotechnical workshop at the YMCA and burn it down.'

Scarborough College's gym/hall, in contrast, quickly came to be cherished as the Festival's prime performance space. It was in effect a very flexible box, which smoothly accommodated the various permutations in which the technical team could arrange it: end-on, thrust, traverse, and so on. (It would not be uncommon in later years for the venue to be reconfigured at least once during the week of the Festival.) Incredibly, a significant role in the hall's entry into the Festival's heart was played by a flippant throwaway remark by Noises Off editor Stephen Jeffreys. Entering the building for the first time, he remarked, 'It looks like a dolphinarium.' The term was used later that week in the magazine, and took root among the NSDF organisational team to the extent that by the following year, the official Festival programme was referring to it as the Dolph. The name stuck until the new century, when Scarborough College felt it insufficiently respectful; it's now much more prosaically known as New Hall.

In any case, the 1990 Festival was imbued with a feeling of freshness. It was also something of a vintage year for stars-in-the-making productions. Leicester Polytechnic (now De Montfort University) brought two productions, Cold Comfort and The Hypochondriac, with a company including actor Alex Lowe, actor/physical performer Miltos Yerolemou and actor/director Justin Chadwick, who a bare year later would star in Hanif Kureishi's film London Kills Me (along with one of 1991's Festival judges, Fiona Shaw). Cambridge University's deconstruction On Hamlet featured actor/comedian Ben Miller, Dominic Cavendish who now reviews theatre for the Daily Telegraph, and writer/director David Farr.

Other names receiving early exposure in 1990 included Tim Fountain, writer of the Hull University production Morning Has Broken, and 'Biyi Bandele-Thomas (who has since dropped the apostrophe and the Thomas), author of the International Student Playscript Competition winner Rain, which had won in 1988 but had to wait till 1990 to receive a rehearsed reading at the Festival.

Ben Miller in Cambridge University's *On Hamlet*

NSDF has a way about it of proving crucial to the shape of individuals' lives. In 1990 the focus of this effect was a Scunthorpe teacher: Doncaster-born Richard Cameron of Thomas Sumpter School. His 1990 offering, Can't Stand Up For Falling Down, proved viscerally, harrowingly powerful. (I remember dozens of us leaping to our feet to give it an ovation at the dramatic climax some two minutes before the actual ending.) Richard won the Sunday Times Playwriting Award for a record third time, the remarkable Joanne Wootton received a commendation for her acting, and the production was adopted by sister organisation the National Student Theatre Company to be produced that August in Edinburgh. During that run, it won the 1990 Theatre Award then given by the Independent for an outstanding new work on the Edinburgh Fringe, which in turn secured it an autumn run at London's Hampstead Theatre. Such was the overall success of the production that Richard gave up his teaching job to concentrate on playwriting; he has since had half a dozen plays premiere at London's Bush Theatre, and a couple of West End runs into

The original cast of *Can't Stand Up For Falling Down*
(left to right: Deborah Kilner, Joanne Wootton, Donna Stones)

Photograph © Allan Titmuss

the bargain. Can't Stand Up... itself became a modern classic, to the extent that a decade later, another production of it was selected for the Festival, by a company who had no idea at the time that they were in effect bringing it back home.

A more bizarre career start came in the form of An Evening With André Boloque, a cabaret show given a single performance, 'out of competition'. It was astoundingly dreadful. Performer Andrew Clover misjudged the amount of preparation he needed to do, was attacked en route to the venue, and found himself hitting in performance on too few and too squalid riffs. By the end of the hour, only around a third of the original audience remained. Clover, though, returned to the Festival the following year, showed his mettle by strolling off with the Student Critics' Award, then went into acting (including a role in the original production of Mark Ravenhill's Shopping and Fucking) before returning to comedy with much the same kind of attitude as Monsieur Boloque, but much more adroitly handled.

Other 1990 memories include the first performance of the Angela Brazil-style spoof The Big Book for Girls, subsequently rewritten and adopted as the mid-1990s signature production of the NSTC; student Oliver Couzens finding himself a pariah for daring to suggest in a discussion that public funding might not be the way

It remains a blur, the 1990 drama Festival. I was a second year English student and I was in love. My mind was elsewhere and I didn't take notes. I remember being impressed by Scarborough, its double-nature – cliff-top town and arcade-lined beach – and struck by its desolation. I played Claudius in David Farr's production of *Hamlet*, which had been substantially cut, allowing for the addition of a fancifully fragmented second half – lines from T S Eliot and other quotations delivered in handmade masks – which no one in the cast quite understood – but even then Farr somehow had the knack of persuading people to trust him. Our Hamlet – Ben Miller – was clearly very good, and it was strange suddenly being in a public environment in which that was commented upon, far outside the cosy thespian confines of Cambridge. I wasn't very good – or at least I wasn't nearly vicious enough – and a critic called Ian Shuttleworth pointed this out. It was the beginning of the end of my flirtation with the idea of being an actor. With hindsight, I'm grateful he speeded up the process – although it also left me with a lasting memory of what it's like to be on the receiving end of a negative notice. As for becoming a professional reviewer, that thought hadn't even entered on the horizon yet. I remember Robert Hewison giving a talk at the Stephen Joseph Theatre (how everyone loved talking about 'in-the-round' spaces) – and he seemed like an impossibly distinguished figure. John Godber spoke there, too – rising heavily to his feet, and apologising for being late, on account of having just 'been for a pizza'. Perhaps he was still eating pizza when he spoke. The recollection is hazy, but whenever I go back to the SJT – which is quite often for the *Telegraph* – I think of Godber, his pizza, and being young.
Dominic Cavendish

Photograph © Allan Titmuss

1991

The Spa Centre played a much greater part in 1991's NSDF, as it has done ever since. A magnificent Victorian entertainment centre – now, inevitably, a conference centre – it boasts venues for workshops, discussions, performances, socialising, magazine production (in the marvellous, if chilly, glass-fronted 'Vitadome', normally a tea-room) and the like all under one roof. It has proved a natural hub for the Festival; when a Spa barman said, 'This is the best week of the year,' it's uncertain whether he was referring to enjoyment or takings.

The year's faces of the future included actor Matthew Dunster (first seen aged 16 in 1988's Orphans, now back as a student in a production of John Godber's Bouncers), actress Lena Headey in The Coca-Cola Dragon, a show about Vietnam from Shelley High School in Huddersfield, and director Indhu Rubasingham with a production of Clare McIntyre's Low Level Panic. The Festival also saw the first appearance in discussion and in print from a serious young Donna Munday, who subsequently went on to

for theatre to operate; and the first ever episode of what was to become a Noises Off signature, the parody serial, in this case the Hunter S Thompson burlesque Fear and Loathing in Scarborough.

Noises Off itself was under new management: Stephen Jeffreys and Nick Phillips, spotting an energetic and above all gullible candidate, made off while the going was good, leaving a surprised Ian Shuttleworth in titular charge at only his fourth Festival, with the much more experienced Lon David and Gaie Sebold doing most of the actual work on the production and editorial fronts respectively.

Top: Dartington College's *The Big Book for Girls*, 1990
Right: *Bouncers* (Matthew Dunster and Peter Machen), 1991

Photograph © Allan Titmuss

Schools have always had a mixed reception at the NSDF. Often it is one of surprise that they should have got there at all. Often it is a patronising, 'Well that was very good...for a school play!' Occasionally a hostile 'The NSDF is no place for a school play!'

It cannot be denied that school productions have played an important part in the Festival. This is hardly surprising, given careful consideration. School companies have many advantages over student companies. They often have adult directors, with many years' experience. They have a support structure of professional musicians and artists, while the performers themselves are often only a year or two away from university/college. Usually they have a bigger budget, good facilities and help with the logistics of touring. Hence the enormous success of such productions as *Ruddigore* (1992), Tony Grounds' *Holiday in the Sun* (1986) and Sally Mackie's *Godspell* (1989).

In recent years schemes like Shell Connections, Shakespeare for Schools and the NAYT have helped to lift the standard of school and youth theatre. Directors are better trained, design and technical standards are rising and performers have more opportunity to develop as school drama departments adopt Arts Council guidelines and teacher training improves. In short, given a level playing field, school and youth theatre is likely to have an even greater influence on the NSDF over the coming years.

There may be fears that the rise in school companies may herald a plague of school entries to the Festival. In the eyes of some this may threaten to devalue the Festival because, in these days of selling education, a place in the NSDF finals is a good marketing point for a college drama department to advertise, especially if it is there alongside Oxford, Cambridge, RADA, Central or LIPA, not so good alongside Cleckheckmondwike Secondary.

However there are benefits to catching them young. One of the beneficial spin-offs of having school students at the Festival is that the young people are so enthused, their experiences usually so good, that they become ambassadors for the NSDF when they do, eventually, go to college/university. There have been many examples of School students returning with their university companies and even of ex-school entrants returning later, as teachers, with their own school parties.

Stephen Downs
(former Head of Drama at Shelley High School, thrice NSDF Finalists)

sections of the Fest and given for outstanding contribution to the week overall, went to Stranmillis College, Belfast, whose impressionistic piece Making The Number Up was one of the hits of the week. Stranmillis contingents were to become increasingly involved in the next few years.

managerial stints at the Royal Court and Stoll Moss Theatres before taking up her current position as Chief Executive of Northampton Theatres.

The oldest play at the Festival dated from 1974. New work included the sharply staged Morons, which equally sharply divided opinions: Andrew Clover opined in Noises Off that, 'It was a self-dismantling robot… My objection is not that it was so stupid, but that it was so timidly stupid.' Eric Prince returned, though not quite at his best, with the nevertheless atmospheric In the Ruins of Song. However, the Sunday Times Playwriting Award was withheld that year by the panel of regular chairman Robert Hewison, director Phyllida Lloyd and actor Fiona Shaw ('If we have a crash with that car we'll lose two theatrical geniuses and Robert Hewison,' remarked Tim Fountain). The Royal Insurance award, to a company chosen by a panel drawn from all

Top: Stanmillis College Belfast's *Making the Number Up*

Right: Molière's *The Hypochondriac*
(including Miltos Yerolemou, centre, and Alex Lowe, bottom right)

Photograph © Allan Titmuss

1992

Ruddigore

To begin at the end of the 1992 Festival: the final night's ad hoc cabaret boasted the usual gamut of semi-impressive to outright tragic acts, and one breathtaking one. A 15-year-old from Shelley High School's Many Rivers company, having attended Huw Thomas' workshops on stand-up comedy, utterly stormed even as drunken and unforgiving a crowd as this one composed of several hundred teenagers on the pull. His set was about being an inadequate but smart teen. His name was Daniel Kitson. Ten years later, in Edinburgh, those of us who'd seen his beginnings were entirely unsurprised when he won the Perrier Comedy Award.

Several careers were launched by the company from Bretton Hall responsible for the aggressive, confrontational Face to Face. This was the birth of John Keates' company fecund THEATRE, which would produce several non-linear, multimedia shows of varying degrees of interest over the next several years; the company here also included actor Dominic Coleman and Mandy Jones, who as Amanda

Lawrence has recently and brilliantly reinvented herself post-fecund as a visual/physical comic performer. Face to Face garnered an award for Best Devised Work from judges Robert Hewison, Phyllida Lloyd and short-notice replacement Brian Cox. Robert Hewison remembers:

> The worst problem for the Artistic Director is getting someone to commit to being a judge. Busy actors don't like to tie themselves down. I remember that in 1992 there was a week to go and we were still short of a judge. I went to review a show at the Swan in Stratford and I found myself sitting next to Brian Cox, who I had interviewed at the Hay on Wye literary festival. Was he doing anything the following week? He wasn't, and he made a terrific judge.

The Cambridge company behind Goddess included Emily Gray, now artistic director of Trestle Theatre Company, and Laurie Sansom, who has never quite managed to get away from Scarborough: after several years as an NSDF selector he's now also Alan Ayckbourn's directorial lieutenant at the Stephen Joseph. Two Into One, from Leeds, was performed by subsequent Festival selector Vanessa Bray and Elizabeth Besbrode, now of physical theatre company Leikin Loppu. A guest production arrived from recently-independent Lithuania, to find themselves facing a mood of black despair amongst young Britons at a Festival held only a few days after John Major's general election victory.

In the midst of all this, it might seem improbable that the hit of the Festival would be a Gilbert and Sullivan production from a Roman Catholic high school in Manchester. But Ruddigore, by St Mary's in Tyldesley, had an infectious joy about it: just the right amount of irreverence which informs the best G&S productions, a clutch of excellent performances, and a style which perfectly suited (as scarcely any shows ever do) the inflexible Victorian proscenium arch space of the Spa Theatre. Clive Wolfe remembers the show as one of the greatest highlights of the 48 Festivals that he has attended, and St Mary's took the judges' award for best production and best actor.

Above: fecund THEATRE's inaugural show *Face to Face*
(with Dominic Coleman), 1992
Above right: Andrea Dougherty in *Face Licker Come Home*, 1993

1993

Glasgow University's production of Brian Friel's Translations was recognised at the time as a strong show, but only with hindsight has the full impressive nature of the company grown apparent. It boasted a director who subsequently

found fame as a writer (Nicola McCartney, who sometimes looks as if she's obliged by law to supply sixty per cent of all new plays in Scotland), an actor who later became a director (John Tiffany, most associated with the Traverse Theatre), and another actor who went on to become Director with a capital D: Andrew Loretto, who took over the Artistic Directorship of NSDF ten years later. Andrew even wrote a couple of pieces for Noises Off, one of which asked, 'Who could fail to be won over by Dougherty's all embracing smile and generosity of spirit?' True to his own judgement, a decade later he appointed Andrea Dougherty, now Andrea Grimason, as a Festival selector. In 1993, though, she was not only a remarkable performer in the solo piece Face Licker Come Home (from Stranmillis), but was simply the face of the Festival, more ubiquitous and enthusiastic than many a much larger company and sunnier than the summery weather that always seems to bless the final day of NSDF at Scarborough even after the bleakest of preceding weeks.

Laurie Sansom's 1993 production, Lorca's Blood Wedding, was less well received: Festival judge Fiona Shaw came rushing out of the performance to find me in the bar and trilled mischievously, 'I have an essay title for you: "Class and the Classics." How long do I have to write it?' She never delivered her copy. Indeed, the overall standard of criticism in print that year was thin, and the student critic's award, newly renamed in honour of the late Sir Harold Hobson, was not bestowed. Its 1992 winner (and 1991 International Student Playscript Competition winner) Robert Shearman, returned, though, to win the Sunday

Top: Richard Hurst's *Ripley Bogle*

Bottom: *Talking Birds* (Dave Lamb, Gordon Southern)

Times Playwriting Award for his bleak Nazi-Christmas fable Easy Laughter, on the strength of which he received a commission from Alan Ayckbourn that set off his professional writing career.

An NSDF fringe show saw the return of 1980s Festival discoveries Miles & Millner; the rest of the world has since caught up with Tom Miles, who reverted to his real name Richard Thomas and nurtured his idea for Jerry Springer – the Opera. Radio 4's arts programme Kaleidoscope came up to cover the Festival: when presenter Robert Dawson Scott tried to round off a 24-hour stint by interviewing Noises Off editor Ian Shuttleworth at 3 am in the Noises Off office, it was hard to gauge which of the two was in a more advanced state of meltdown. After the electoral gloom of 1992, the great debate in the magazine this year was on an altogether more cultural matter: 'ass' or 'arse'? The Anglo-Saxon lobby rightly carried the day.

1993 also saw the welcome breaking of a reluctant tradition. The Festival's most cherished award had long been the Buzz Goodbody Award for a director. Its name was taken seriously: successive panels of judges considered it such an accolade that it could in effect only be given to a director whose talent and flair could stand comparison with the woman in whose memory it was named, and consequently it was in fact seldom awarded – never, in my experience as an NSDF attendee since 1988. This year, however, Andrew Wilford, from the North Riding College 'home team', received the award for his oblique, sometimes indulgent but phenomenally realised original production Sandcastle.

But the year's most lasting memory is of the final night, when the magic that NSDF can spontaneously generate came together wondrously. After the cabaret/disco closed down, the musical accompanists from a couple of shows gained access to the Spa Centre's Sun Court and, in moonlight and with the sea behind them, began a fiddle-playing jam session. A crowd gathered…a fire-juggler materialised…by the time the night was over, a proposal of marriage had been made and accepted. Sometimes the plays themselves are distinctly secondary to what the Festival is about.

1994

A record 120 shows were entered for the 1994 Festival, and for the first time a majority of Festgoers were not involved with a selected production. Although Laurie Sansom was, again, twice. Other returnees included Daniel Kitson, and Andrea Dougherty, directing her own play Fire Escape and winning that year's Smith Award endowed by the American university of the same name. New arrivals included actor Mark Rice-Oxley, Sacha Wares (later to make a career as a director, most recently of the hit verbatim drama Guantanamo) and playwright Robert Hamilton, in the first of three appearances in successive years. He would win the Sunday Times Playwriting Award in 1995 and 1996, but judges Robert Hewison, Nick Phillips and Josette Simon felt unable to bestow it on anyone this year; the Buzz Goodbody award, too, was once again withheld after its brief airing the previous year. A particularly strong company from Middlesex, who presented the John Wright-influenced meditation on war She'll Be Coming Round The Mountain, included actors Emma Rydal (née Powell), Jason Thorpe and Phoebe Soteriades.

Unsurprisingly, debate about wider issues continued to focus on funding. Protests came in particular from students at the Central School of Speech and Drama, worried and incensed that their institution appeared to be turning itself into a qualification and income factory rather than a training conservatoire. Elsewhere, a casual usage in discussion by Robert Hewison led to 'meretricious' becoming the word of the Festival. Noises Off conducted a vox pop to see how many people knew what it in fact meant; one flippant reply was, 'It's the noise a horse makes when it sneezes.'

> **Scarborough has always had a techie picnic, struggling against inclement weather and being shifted in location from the castle, to the beach and even the Ocean room foyer. Catering whilst in a permanent Festival location has become rather well organised, with crew regularly sitting down to hot meals... memories which go back further seem to mostly involve endless baked beans, and the ordering of takeaway pizza.**
> **Jo Horrobin (with help from Jan Sayer, Robert Edenborough and H)**

Left: *She'll Be Coming Round the Mountain*
Above: *Going Up* (Natasha Pollard, left, Rosanna Lowe)

Photograph © Allan Titmuss

1995

The 40th NSDF in 1995 was a time to celebrate, but also to take stock. Despite the Festival's longevity and a number of long-standing sponsors, its existence from year to year was still ultimately a matter of patchworking funding together on a one-off basis. In that year's first issue of Noises Off, vice-editor Gaie Sebold wrote:

> What have we to celebrate? This is the 40th NSDF. The Festival Has Survived… It is worrying that the Festival has to fight for every inch. Worrying? Hell, it's shameful. In a truly civilised country, those who create and run a resource like this would be on the Civil List by now. Instead, they are often broke, tired and largely unacknowledged except by their equally broke and exhausted peers. But it's still going. It runs on love, dedication and the kind of energy expenditure that could power New York.

Noises Off also included articles by Robert MacLennan of the Liberal Democrats and Shadow Heritage Secretary Chris Smith on the state of the arts; the third day carried an otherwise blank page, which constituted Secretary of State Stephen Dorrell's response in the four weeks between request and publication.

1990's Hamlet Ben Miller returned as a workshop leader. Richard Hurst won the Buzz Goodbody Award for the

Photograph © Allan Titmuss

Above: The late Kenn Price with Dave Maybrick in *Violent Night*
Above right: Shakespeare's *Pericles, Prince of Tyre*

Welsh College of Music and Drama's production Violent Night, a tense two-hander between a couple of night security guards; sadly, writer and actor Kenn (Griffin) Price would die in his mid-forties only a few years later, before fully realising his late flowering in theatre.

In a radical acknowledgement, the Harold Hobson Award was given to long-time Noises Off stalwart Paul Arendt for his mordant graphics as well as his writing.

NOFF's Production Editor Lon David retired from the 'bijou Festmag', but thankfully not from Festivalgoing.

NSDF débuts were made by director Erica Whyman (who subsequently took the helm of London's Gate Theatre) and a company from Leeds University including Jon Spooner, Liz Margee and Chris Thorpe who would later become linchpins of Unlimited Theatre. That year also saw a warmly received guest production, Soundjata from the University of Cape Town.

The Festival Director's Award, made by Clive Wolfe in personal acknowledgement of outstanding long-term contribution to NSDF, went to Steven Downs of Shelley High School.

A couple of NSDF's more eccentric traditions began this year. One, in which the prizes for the Festival 'pub quiz' (which supplanted a previous panel-based format in 1993) are regularly and inventively stolen by the tech team, never ceases to bemuse. The other came to be a victim of its own success. One night Noises Off editor Ian Shuttleworth, bored of just calling 'Copy deadline!' at 1.30 am, sang it instead, to thrashed guitar accompaniment and the tune of The Sex Pistols' 'Anarchy In The UK' ('I am an antichrist / I am a journalist…'). Within days, the copy deadline song had become such a cult that crowds would roll up to the NOFFice after the late-night bar closed, just to hear the editorial team parody another rock standard. Over the next few years 'Wonderwall', 'Pinball Wizard' and 'I Heard It Through the Grapevine' were just a few of the classics massacred by Shuttleworth and associates. In the end it became more trouble than it was worth. Ah, but few who heard the final night's massed rendition of 'Bohemian Rhapsody' ('Ben Miller… No!') will ever forget it. Try as they might.

The 40th-Fest milestone was celebrated with a lavish event at the Holbeck Hall Hotel on Scarborough's South Cliff; attendees included Simon Russell Beale, John Godber and Jason Isaacs. Less than a month later, the whole country knew Holbeck Hall, as the media reported the cliff beside it crumbling little by little, day by day, until finally the hotel tumbled into the North Sea, beginning with the conservatory where we'd so recently been making merry. NSDF continues to deny all responsibility.

Photograph © Allan Titmuss

Jacqueline Haigh in *The Madwoman in the Attic*, directed by Erica Whyman

1996

Seventeen plays were selected for NSDF 1996, with a total running time of over 25 hours – the greatest amount of stage time since the 20- and 21-show excesses respectively of Cambridge in 1988 and 1989. They included an epic production of Joshua Sobol's Ghetto from Warwick University, a bizarre solo Hamlet from Nathan Evans of Oxford University, and a staging of Maria Irene Fornes' The Danube from Manchester Metropolitan University, which was at once hilarious and harrowing, as director Emma Hewitt had her cast gradually douse themselves in flour to signify nuclear fallout. In Hull University's production of Ionesco's The Bald Prima Donna came an early sign that Sam Troughton would follow father David and grandfather Patrick as a respected actor.

For once, the type and standard of criticism in daily discussions and in Noises Off itself became an issue. On the one hand, a certain tendency was evinced towards mealy-

Warwick University's *Ghetto*

Photograph © Allan Titmuss

I first attended the NSDF in 1994 when my friends and I volunteered to be part of the front of house teams. I was instantly hooked. It was the first time I'd encountered a sense of professional responsibility, and I knew that if such a role existed I'd eventually love my 'proper' job to have the same kind of buzz. In 1996 I was Local Organiser and it remains one of the best weeks of my life. Co-ordinating with people all over the country during the months leading up to the Festival week and getting to know so many talented, funny and passionate people was extraordinary. During the week itself, I would aim to be at the Spa by 8.30am to ensure everything was set up in the Box Office, reception and for the workshops and I'd meet with Clive to discuss anything that had materialised over night, having usually left *Noises Off* at about 4am. Somehow, like most people including Clive, I survived on just over three hours sleep per night all week.

In the final year of my degree I was fortunate enough to win the student administration award, which gave me the opportunity to work at the National. There is no doubt that the experience I gained from being part of the NSDF and working for Clive has been the foundation of my career and something I will always cherish and value enormously.

Sarah Nicholson

mouthed wimp-outs. On the other, vitriol was heaped on the University of Kent at Canterbury's production of Cabaret, in which everything went wrong; admirably, the company knew this and explained in detail, with the result that instead of being seen as a disaster in itself, the show came to be recognised as an object lesson in the difficulties of transferring a production from a home venue to an entirely unfamiliar Scarborough space with four weeks'

notice and only a matter of hours to run technical and dress rehearsals in situ.

Judges Robert Hewison and Stephen Jeffreys were joined by Lithuanian-born actress Ingeborga Dapkunaite, who took in good part Noises Off's daily anagrams of her name including 'OK adapting aubergine', 'Unkind to a garbage pie' and 'Broken guinea-pig data'. One of their ad hoc awards carried the citation 'for originality and completely off-the-wall lunacy' to Tim Glover of Hull for All the World's a Biscuit, a sensitive yet humorous play about Asperger's syndrome; he would top it the following year with Not Enough Points on the Chicken, about the neurological oddity of synaesthesia.

Some of the most bizarrely lingering memories of NSDF week can consist of one- or two-liners testifying to the amount of mental frazzlement and/or lateral thinking that goes on at such a non-stop jamboree. Gems this year included: 'Stephen and I are holding a session on organisation tomorrow morning' – 'Tomorrow afternoon, actually, Andrea'; and the backstage exchange: 'Who turned on the workers?' – 'Karl Marx, wasn't it?'

Above: Robert Hamilton's *The Interview*

Below: *Hamlet*

Shortly after NSDF 1996, the new Stephen Joseph Theatre opened in Scarborough. Beautifully converted from the town's old art deco Odeon cinema and funded in part by a six-figure donation from Alan Ayckbourn himself, the new SJT boasted both an enhanced version of its traditional in-the-round space and an end-on venue, the McCarthy Theatre. Consequently, Sir Alan made both spaces available to NSDF in 1997, both for productions and for daily discussions, which finally found a perfect venue in the Round auditorium.

In another advance, the growing complexity of enabling all holders of subscription tickets to see performances of

every show was addressed by introducing a number of specific 'routes' through the week. One's route, of course, came to be regarded as a status symbol; most prized was the red route as taken by the Festival judges, who this year included guests Janet Dale and Tim Pigott-Smith.

The rationalisation of the ticketing system was just one the advances pioneered by Iain Ormsby-Knox, who, in this final phase of Clive's directorship, provided much of the vision and drive which kept the Festival expanding and improving. The results of his determination and inventiveness still benefit Festivalgoers to this day.

It was a solid rather than a vintage year show-wise, including another epic from Warwick with Tony Kushner's Angels in America, two productions of Jim Cartwright's Two (differing radically in script cuts and duration, they became known flippantly as 'Two Short' and 'Two Long'), a brave stab by Middlesex University at staging Herman Melville's Moby Dick, and in a year of adaptations and deconstructions, the laurel went to a site-specific Icelandic-themed version of Hamlet, called Amlodi's Journey, which used several spaces including one hung entirely with sides of meat. A production of Decadence led Paul Arendt to formulate the magnificent axiom: 'Nobody does Berkoff except students and Berkoff.'

At another point during the week, I joined the gradual exodus from a mind-numbingly tedious production of Waiting for Godot to take refuge in the Noises Off office,

Above: *Nobody Here But Us Chickens*
Above right: *Amlodi's Journey*

90

only to find I'd been beaten to it by fugitive judge Tim Pigott-Smith, pleading, 'Don't tell anyone I'm here!'

Leeds University's Sex and Death gave early exposure to actor John Hopkins and writer John Donnelly. However, the most significant discovery was the winner of the year's Harold Hobson award, then a recent Cambridge graduate but very soon afterwards a writer on the Guardian, where she is now reviews editor: Maddy Costa.

Hardboard is an NSDF way of life – most of the venues are covered in sheets of the stuff, which must be carefully stored from one year to the next, often in near inaccessible locations. Few of us involved will forget the ordeal of stacking hundreds of sheets beneath Scarborough College Hall stage. *Moby Dick* in 1997 covered the hardboard floor in the Dolphinarium with water, creating a wonderful concentric circle design with powder paint. Unfortunately the water stubbornly refused to dry and hairdryers had to be brought from around Scarborough to try and dry the floor before focusing could begin. Hardboard has also been used to black out windows, although in 1990 it was decided that black bin bags could be used instead – each show in the Dolphinarium that year accompanied by a gentle rustling in the breeze.

Jo Horrobin (with help from Jan Sayer, Robert Edenborough and H)

John Hopkins (centre) in *A Short Play About Sex and Death*

Photograph © Allan Titmuss

1998

The expansion of the Festival community beyond those attending with selected productions continued: by 1998, more than 75 per cent of Festgoers were unattached to shows. Access (in the physical rather than the social or ethnic sense), a recurrent issue, continued to be improved with the introduction of Midland Bank bursaries to enable disabled students to attend. Robert Hewison was joined on the judging troika by John Godber and Cathy Tyson. Actor and director Mark Bowden, who became known at NSDF as 'the man with the hair of a woman' and also the owner of an improbable collection of loud clothing, made his début as moderator of the daily discussions.

1997's roster of workshop leaders, which had included Sandi Toksvig, Stephen Daldry and Mark Ravenhill, was at least equalled by a bill including Annabel Arden, Timothy West, Emily Gray and Ken Campbell. Campbell, irrepressible as ever, brought to the Festival a guest production of Macbeth translated into Pidgin as Makbed

blong Willum Sekspia performed by a company of Lamda students and co-directed by Nikki Amuka-Bird. Lady M's 'Come, you spirits/that tend on mortal thoughts: unsex me here' became 'Seten, tekem mi hambag!' Explained Campbell: 'Hambag is the dirtiest word there is in Pidgin; not advisable to tour The Importance of Being Earnest around the Pacific islands…'. Another guest production was a remarkable puppet show by 13-year-old Hungarian Balaz Lippai, while the rehearsed reading of 1997's ISPC winner The Square Root of Minus One introduced the world at large to the smart, mordant playwriting talents of Yale and Oxford alumnus Peter Morris, subsequently to attract notoriety with his alleged 'James Bulger play' The Age of Consent and a light operetta about British fascism A Million Hearts for Mosley.

The overall complexion of Festival shows is never predictable. Some years it will tend strongly towards original or recent plays; 1998, in contrast, saw a clutch of established pieces such as Under Milk Wood, Pinter's The Dwarfs and a special revision by David Edgar of his Ball Boys. It also included Guys and Dolls from Exeter University, which alas fell prey to many of the same transfer problems as Canterbury's Cabaret, and what at the time seemed a contemporary classic but is now revealed as a flash-in-the-

Left and below: Ken Campbell's *Pidgin Makbed*

pan fad, Harry Gibson's stage adaptation of Irvine Welsh's *Trainspotting*.

This last led to one of the great *Noises Off* cover designs of all time, in which the Festival director's head was PhotoShopped onto the image of Ewan McGregor's Renton emerging from a toilet bowl and accompanied by a rewrite of the character's 'Choose life' speech:

Choose Clive… Choose exhaustion. Choose pimply gits in leggings…

The design was reprised two years later as a T-shirt design to bid Clive farewell. At the end of the 1998 Festival, it was announced that he had been diagnosed with Parkinson's Disease, and as a result would be retiring from the Directorship at the end of NSDF 2000. Immediately, the tributes began pouring in for a man who had been with the Festival literally since Year One, and thankfully has continued since as honorary president. Another sad departure was the retirement after 14 years of *Noises Off*'s vice-editor and latterly co-editor Gaie Sebold.

Top: Ashley Alymann in LIPA's *Storyteller*

Bottom: Cambridge University's *City Haunts*

1999

Another record was set in 1999, with 133 shows entered, from which 16 were selected: mostly extant works, but probably the most eclectic selection in my NSDF experience. Plays produced were written by Arthur Miller (A View From the Bridge, featuring Hattie Morahan), Samuel Beckett, David Hare, John Godber and Antonin Artaud; also by Stewart Harcourt, who had been a performer in NSDF 1990's Royal Insurance Award-winner Futurist Love in the Apple, and a début by Amy Rosenthal, daughter of Jack Rosenthal and Maureen Lipman.

Long-time Festival stalwarts the Liverpool Institute of Performing Arts raised eyebrows when they equalled the all-time record with four shows selected. Accusations of favouritism were levelled, since Clive's Festival lieutenant Iain Ormsby-Knox was also in a senior teaching position at LIPA. As often, it needed to be explained that part of the LIPA course involved requiring groups of students to stage a production entirely independent of institutional help, including securing all the funding themselves. This year's

shows were Harcourt's Somogyi's Monologue, Godber's Teechers, A R Gurney's neglected absurdist miniature The Problem and the Heather Brothers' musical A Slice Of Saturday Night, which predictably proved the feelgood hit of the Fest and was recognised as such with an award for musical ensemble from the judging panel of Robert Hewison, Annie Castledine and Emma Fielding. Workshop leaders this year also included Henry Goodman and Simon McBurney.

The 1999 Festival saw the welcome beginning of a link with the Bush Theatre, which continues to this day, commenced with director Mike Bradwell puckishly teaching one hapless company a practical lesson. Middlesex University's These Colours, about football terrace violence, began with the audience being foul-mouthedly shepherded into the in-the-round Westwood space ('Get in there, you cunts!' etc.). Once in, we were expected to huddle on the stage whilst the performers harangued us from the banks of seating on all four sides. Mike took a seat halfway up one bank.

> ACTOR: Get down there, you bastard!
>
> MIKE: (Calmly.) No.
>
> ACTOR, out of his depth, calls a comrade over; more expletives; MIKE immovable, plays his trump card:
>
> Say please.
>
> ACTORS sheepishly comply.

The point being that once you, as a performer, break the usual actor/audience relationship and remake it along such stark lines, you need to be prepared for the punters to take up the challenge and screw up your best-laid plans.

Like young Britain in general, student drama had entered the 1990s with one kind of political disillusionment and ended the decade with another. In 1990, voicing opposition to Thatcher had become so much of a habit that chants of 'Maggie, Maggie, Maggie, out, out, out!' scarcely registered above the background noise; yet there was no sense that such opposition would actually achieve anything, even six months before she was finally ousted. By 1999, having

---

We were the opening show of the Festival, and were therefore the first that year to experience the no-holds-barred post-show discussion. Although nerve-wracking, it was so valuable to hear where people felt we'd succeeded and what aspects of the production had failed, and I've not encountered that kind of collective constructive feedback since. There was some really impressive and varied work that year – I remember an amazing production inspired by Artaud's Theatre of Cruelty – and so it was very exciting when Rosanna Lavelle and I both got given Outstanding Performance awards. It was a recognition that the work we were all doing could stand up to professional judgement, and was a real confidence booster. I put it on my CV so it's often a talking point in auditions.

Hattie Morahan

experienced a Labour government which gave no indication of being any more in touch with their concerns, the generation's theatre work seemed more directed towards broader, global issues than domestic Westminster-influenced ones. There were even signs of a return to the old notion that 'the personal is political'.

One of the most powerful indicators of how young people's attitudes had changed in this respect came with Bristol University's production of David Hare's The Absence of War. Barely five years after its première, director Roland Smith and his company responded naturally to the play as if it were not the tragedy of a Labour party leader who refused to countenance playing the spin game out of strongly held principles, but the far less weighty misfortune of a man too naïve to recognise its central place in the political machine. Nevertheless, the show worked strongly on its own terms and Smith's helmsmanship was acknowledged with the Buzz Goodbody Award.

The highlight of my own Festival career editing *Noises Off* came when...er...sources close to Robert Hewison leaked to us the news that the Cameron Mackintosh Foundation had agreed to fund NSDF to the tune of £150,000 over five years and a new award for musicals. This led to a remarkable night in the NOFFice when I had to pretend that a normal issue was being put together, whilst all the time being huddled in a corner with Robert and Stephen Jeffreys assembling a cover which was painstakingly (let's be honest: paranoiacally) vetted to contain only moderate irreverence to Mr Producer. (I'm still proud of a cover line about 'The Absence Of Guerre: After being believed dead for years, the Labour Party comes home... But is it the real Labour Party?') Then, at around 4.30 am, I got to utter, for probably the only time in my professional life, one of the classic lines of print journalism: 'Hold the front page! We're making it over!' Nice way to end a decade: scooping *The Sunday Times*.

Ian Shuttleworth

CHAPTER SIX
ANDREW HAYDON

2000
2005

I first became a Festival judge in 1984, and, with the exception of 1988, when my colleague John Peter gave me a break, I have been a judge ever since. To be honest, I didn't know very much about the Festival when I turned up at Bretton Hall that year. I had been a student actor at Oxford in the early 1960s, and some people I had worked with there – future stars Michael York and Michael Elwyn, the director Braham Murray – took part in the Festival, but much to my present regret, the Festival passed me by.

Being a Festival judge came with my job. I had been writing on theatre for *The Sunday Times* since 1981, and since a *Sunday Times* theatre critic, Harold Hobson, had created the Festival, the paper traditionally supplies a judge. In the early years Harold Hobson would do the judging all on his own, and his summings-up are remembered as high drama, ending with a last minute surprise. I have tried to preserve this folk memory, encouraging my fellow-judges to make our own summings-up as dramatic – or at least as entertaining – as the shows we have seen.

I understand that when Bernard Levin was a judge he reserved the right to walk out after the first act of an entered production, or even not to go at all, so the burden was shared with others. For the two years before I started James Fenton – better known as a poet and librettist – had been chief drama critic on *The Sunday Times* and had impressed everybody at the Festival with his commitment and enthusiasm. Why, he went to see every show.

By 1984 the tradition was established that the *Sunday Times* critic would be joined by two distinguished members of the theatrical profession, ideally, one male, one female, one a director, the other a performer. That year my fellow judges were the actress Sheila Allen and the director Ronald Eyre (who died in 1992). I was immediately confronted with a difficulty I still feel – how do you spend seven intensive days with people whose work you either have criticised, or may have to in the future? It is a question that often comes up in Festival discussions: whose side is the critic on? In this particular case I had not written about Sheila Allen, but I had vivid memories of seeing her in Jane Arden's *Rex Vagina and the Gas Oven* at the Arts Lab in 1969. Sheila was very pleased when I told her what an experience that had been. Ronald Eyre was more tricky, for I had recently panned his production of *St Joan* at the National Theatre. Ronald was too much of a gent ever to mention it.

It was at Bretton Hall in 1984 that the judges jointly decided to change the nature of the awards that we were supposed to be making. There were – and are – certain fixed prizes for categories of person or work. The most prestigious is the Buzz Goodbody Award, set up in memory of the director Mary Ann Goodbody. Rightly, the Buzz Goodbody Award goes to a student director, and such is its prestige that there have been some years when it has not been given. In addition, however, there is a pot of money for prizes that the judges can more or less distribute at will.

It was here that we made some changes in 1984. Previously the awards had tended to follow the traditional 'Best performance by an actor in...', 'Best supporting actress' type of categories, but, as we decided the Festival is as much a celebration as a competition – in fact more a celebration than a competition – we would simply try to acknowledge talent in whatever form it showed itself. So that year there was a Topol Award for a rather good fiddler, and a Captain Scott Award for an actor of considerable talent who struggled on heroically through a mass of technical problems in a disintegrating production. The jokey titles have now gone, but every year we spend as much time trying to craft the right words in the award as we do sorting out who gets what – not that we ever know how much the awards are worth, that is the job of the Artistic Director.

Judging is a serious business, and I have learnt a lot from my fellow judges. Most of the time it has also been very straightforward. Only once have I thought I might have physically to separate two judges. There was one who simply could not make up her mind, and another one ran away, disturbed by having to pass opinions on fellow actors. (Fortunately nobody noticed.)

Being a judge is only one part of my job, however. The other is to write an article in *The Sunday Times* about it afterwards. This can be problematic, because I have to stop being a member of the Festival community, taking part in the daily discussions on an equal basis with everyone else, for instance, and revert to being a critic. When I write my review – and it is a review, which means sometimes handing out blame as well as praise – I make it a point of honour to name every production, though with up to twenty shows, and limited space, that takes ingenuity. One year the sub-editors cut a four-line paragraph, and three shows bit the dust, expunged from history. I have now written my report 19 times – except that it is never the same review, because the work can be so varied, anything from a full scale production of *Guys and Dolls* from Exeter in 1998 that cost £10,000 just to bring to the Festival, to the exquisite precision of Julia Bardsley and Phelim McDermott's *Cupboard Man* in 1985. If I do have a hobbyhorse, it is the reluctance of students to tackle classic texts like Shakespeare. They do try, of course, but somehow the language of classical theatre and its oral equivalent, the actor's voice, are neglected elements in contemporary student drama.

One reason for that may be the constant struggle that student drama has to survive. Looking back over my old reviews I see constant references to the pressures exerted by the curriculum, at school and university, by the lack of financial support, the growing costs of putting on shows and the general discouragement of creativity by both Conservative and Labour governments. The Festival tries to be a flagship, not because some Festgoers will become future professionals, but because it is a community where theatre is celebrated, and we are all active citizens. It is healthy to have to answer the question, Whose side is the critic on? My answer is that I am on the side of theatre. Just as long as it is good.

Robert Hewison

2000

The 45th NSDF was Clive Wolfe's last as Festival Director. His achievements cannot be overstated; from 1968, when he was appointed administrator, he worked constantly through financial crisis after financial crisis, always finding a way to make it possible for the Festival to continue. Clive himself would be the first to admit that he lacked many of the skills essential for the artistic director's job. Psychologically averse to keeping financial records and a reluctant fundraiser, he was a survivor of the age of amateurs into the age of professionals – and a good advertisement for it. His most important asset was his love of the NSDF. In 1956 the Festival changed his life so he wanted it to change other people's. To keep that simple philosophy alive, he was willing to work all hours, to drive the length and breadth of the country and to accept very little in the way of financial reward. He developed sensitive antennae. On the numerous occasions when the Festival was threatened, he always found the way through the woods. When the stakes were high he had the knack of forming the helpful alliance, of making the correct threat, of leaping intuitively to the right decision. In his time he had been a useful boxer and a very dangerous opponent at the card table – and both disciplines were evident in the way he worked. He was pugnacious, he had stamina and he calculated well under pressure. When the Festival staged a farewell to him and Pat, the anecdotes were numerous and fuelled with deep affection. Without him, the Festival might conceivably have survived into the early 1970's but no further. The achievements recorded in these pages all stem from him.

2000 also saw the departure of Lon David. Clive Wolfe remembers:

> As well as being an actress, singer, 1985 NSDF finalist in Hull's award-winning The Deceits of Memory, and a new solo show The Difference (NSDF 1987), she was a PA/secretary par excellence; intensive researcher; NSDF Selector with an impressive success record; and, in addition to all this, a prime mover in the transformation of Noises Off into a technologically advanced concern. Lon was one of a handful of people who, for some years, helped to keep me from utter despair and office chaos. Twice a week, in 1992–94 and 1998–2000, rain or shine, ill or fit, she drove from Kingston-upon-Thames to the Muswell Hill office to tackle equipment that sometimes varied between just acceptable and dodgy, rather like her boss, whose office defects she overlooked when secretly planning and executing with Stephen Jeffreys the wonderful mini This is Your Life show to celebrate my 30 years as Festival Director at my official retirement in 2000. It was Lon who prepared the statistics that form the basis of information in this book. The Festival owes her a very great deal.
>
> Clive Wolfe

Despite the enormous upheaval that these departures represented for the Festival at large, it was business as usual for the 700-plus students attending NSDF 2000, most of whom had only been alive for two thirds of Clive's 30 years

Below: Welsh College's production of *Silence*
Below right: Peter Morris' *Marge*

The Hunting of the Snark

as Festival Director. The week was marked by two chief qualities, a much-improved standard of work presented, and an avalanche of complaints about the level of criticism received.

The first show of the Festival, an excellent production of Moira Buffini's recent play *Silence* from Welsh College of Music and Drama set the tone for both. Although widely hailed as a perfect combination of script, acting and direction, one student branded the play 'feminism run rampage', while another deemed one of the play's actresses 'not very pretty, but…very annoying'. Understandably, at the discussion of the play, there was some remonstration, with many students wondering outloud whether critics shouldn't just keep their opinions to themselves. The discussion passed off amicably enough, perhaps partially

The only thing worse than watching a really bad piece of theatre is watching a really bad piece of theatre with 300 other people, knowing that it was you who selected it for the Festival. Every year, some of the finest theatrical minds in the country, and the NSDF selection team, do their best to ensure that the invited shows are, at the very least, not really bad. While the Festival correctly upholds the right to fail, no-one wants to be the selector who allows a company to exercise that right.

Selection used to take place at Clive's house in Muswell Hill, with Pat's impressive, extensive and memorable catering to help the team through the day. These days, the selectors meet up in some London theatre or other, and are fuelled only by pre-packed sandwiches and bottled water. The day usually starts with a fag break, before a long shortlist of shows is decided upon. Champions of the best shows, the almost unarguable ones, then speak up for them, and they're accepted for the Festival. Then each of the other shortlisted shows is discussed, and selectors are interrogated as to why they think it should appear. The most useful question is often, 'Would you want to see it again?' or equally, 'Would you want to sit through it again?' Shows are often shelved for discussion later, in a metaphorical fridge, which over the years has developed a metaphorical icebox, a metaphorical salad crisper, and a metaphorical half-can of mouldy baked beans that particularly suspect shows can be put next to. Eventually the contents of the fridge are either accepted or ditched, and only a couple of shows remain in an undecided limbo. Approximately three hours are then spent talking about these shows. Then someone suggests taking neither, and the selectors who've seen the shows look personally affronted. Then someone suggests taking both, and they say, 'Ooh, no, I'm not sure about that.' Another three hours of discussion follow.

Memorably, at Clive's last selection meeting, it was around this time in the evening that he casually dropped a remark into the conversation that people who were at the meeting will never forget; after devoting his life to NSDF, he said, 'Well, it's only student drama.'

Richard Hurst

A selection meeting at Clive Wolfe's house

because it was held in the Spa Centre's Grand Hall with the students sat on the floor assembly-style and with such poor acoustics that it is likely only fifty per cent of the arguments got heard.

The next discussion was less friendly. The venue had changed to the Stephen Joseph Theatre's in-the-round space and there were three shows up for discussion: Oxford University's excellent play Marge, written by 1998's ISPC-winner Peter Morris; Sheffield University's ambitious large-scale devised piece Counterbalance and another new play, Who Wants to Be the Disco King? by Adrian Page. During the discussion it seemed that increasingly only those with criticisms felt moved to speak. By the end, the atmosphere in the discussion was beginning to resemble that of a bear pit. Following that discussion, it began to look as if Clive's last year as Festival Director would echo his first, with student revolt and demands for less competition. A late-night discussion was convened to argue further about negative criticism, with many of the combatants from the morning's discussion, both student and professional, comprising an ad hoc panel. However, by the end of the week, the atmosphere had mellowed considerably, and even the most heated arguments had created an opportunity for the Festivalgoers to better understand each other's positions.

The Festival also saw the first devised piece directed by Warwick University's Dominic LeClerc: Insomnia – an enormously successful and popular marriage of physical theatre, puppetry and multi-media, which explored love and abuse within relationships. Also devised was Middlesex University's striking The Lion, the Witch and a Bag of Chips, which told the story of three mentally ill characters who, in an attempt to hide from their carers in a wardrobe, stumble into the 'real world'. It was both moving and highly inventive theatrically.

A further highlight was a remarkable adaptation by Lu Kemp and Robert Evans of Lewis Carroll's The Hunting of the Snark from Edinburgh University, which closed the Festival – a witty and visually enchanting show whose inventive use of music and musical instruments won the company the inaugural Cameron Mackintosh Award.

2001

For many years, doomsday conversations beginning with the words 'If Clive were to fall under a bus…' had been commonplace. It was Clive himself who, at the suggestion of Robert Hewison, took action by setting up a board of trustees in the last years of his stewardship. The board duly decided that Clive needed to be replaced by two people: Nick Stimson was to be the new Artistic Director of the Festival, assisted, first by Sian Astrop, then by Rachel Williams, as the Festival's administrator.

Nick's stated mission for the Festival was 'to keep the Festival exactly as it always has been, and at the same time change it completely'; a seemingly impossible task, and one that he realised with some élan.

I wanted to keep student theatre at the heart of the Festival. It sounds simple, but in a world of concept-driven arts funding it's not always easy. So often the theatre gets lost. Clive had invented a marvellous format and done an incredible job. All the central things were spot-on. I wanted to keep these, develop them, expand the reach of the Festival, and equip the NSDF for the future. In practical terms this meant creating a model for the NSDF that would allow it to expand and gain extra funding. I also wanted to raise the profile and perception of the Festival. That included establishing permanent offices, recruiting a staff who would bring specific skills to the Festival, and putting the NSDF on a firm financial footing by gaining additional funding. It also meant re-thinking some of the ways the NSDF did what it did.

Like Clive, I wanted a dangerous Festival. A Festival full of surprises. The NSDF needed to continue to take risks, to select work that might be flawed but had moments of genius. Theatre should not be safe. I did not want an NSDF that was a reflection of the worst of professional theatre with anodyne productions. The Festival had to be for today and tomorrow, not yesterday – this has always seemed to be the heart of the Festival. But it also needed to be broad-minded and prepared to explore.

Nick Stimson

Below: *Witness Me*, 2001
Right: *Judith*, 2001

Photograph © Allan Titmuss

Photograph © Allan Titmuss

Following the furore over negative criticism the previous year, the atmosphere of the 2001 Festival was placid by comparison. There were a number of artistic successes through the week, many by students building on their achievements of the previous year. The Dominic LeClerc stable at Warwick University brought two more devised pieces: Dystopia and Witness Me. The latter, which, aesthetically, resembled a ballet about an autopsy, was awarded the Judges' prize for Physical Theatre as well as a Technical Award for Chris Luffingham's outstanding lighting design. Peter Morris returned with a new play: A&R – a chilling reworking of the Faust story, presented by students from Edinburgh University. One of Morris' biggest supporters during the Marge debate of the 2000 Festival, Jenn Lindsay, also returned, bringing a show of her own, The Grandmother Project, from Stanford University, California.

There was an excellent production of Howard Barker's Judith from Cambridge University, directed by Sarah Punshon and a very successful small-scale American musical from LIPA, Falsettoland, directed by Jamie Lloyd. Both Sarah and Jamie were within just a few years to be assisting West Yorkshire Playhouse Director Ian Brown. The newly devised comic play, Pull My Strings, from York was awarded the Festgoer's Award for its massively popular tale of a puppeteer given drama-therapy by his own puppets. While an adaptation of Roddy Doyle's The Woman Who Walked Into Doors from LIPA won both an award for Liz White's virtuoso solo performance and a commendation for the excellent adaptation.

The Festival also saw the now-infamous Atlantica: a play which begins with a number of whales beaching themselves across the world – a cry for help from whale-kind, which is concerned that humanity has 'forgotten how to play' and ends with the hero leaping over the side of his boat and turning into a whale. Factor in dialogue which has since passed into Festival legend: 'Ze, whales, do you sink zey are…evil?' Or, 'Damn it, John, we've got a sperm whale riding shotgun!' And there was a cult 1950s B-movie hit in the making. Whether this was the intention remains a moot point.

Above: Falsettoland, 2001

Left: Pull my Strings, 2001

2002

Halfway between the end of the Festival in 2001 and the start of the next in 2002, the World Trade Centre was destroyed. The impact on the world of both the September 11 attacks on New York and Washington and America's response to them is already well documented. While there were no pieces that dealt directly with 9/11, the Festival's greatest success, a devised piece called Longwave, seemed to articulate the general mood. Its basic premise was a sort-of post apocalyptic vaudeville routine. The three performers continued to cycle through a series of dances and sketches, all the while making apologetic smiles to the audience, as if

Photograph © Allan Titmuss

Longwave

I knew nothing of the National Student Drama Festival when we took my-one act play *Liquid* up to Scarborough in 2002. I had only written the thing to persuade a fellow student deeply involved in the university drama society that I was worth snogging. The NSDF was a hugely chastening, inspiring, opinionated, incestuous experience set by the seaside; rather like if you could climb inside Julie Burchill and hold a festival.

To sit in the Stephen Joseph Theatre and be told by a full auditorium exactly what is wrong with your play. To be bored by a show to the extent you become deeply involved in the game of 'Snake' the audience member in front of you is playing. To be delighted and amazed by a piece of physical theatre by students so much younger than yourself that you can't decide whether to cry with joy or envy. To drink in a bar with practitioners so talented and elusive they would be hard to pin down in their own homes on a Monday night.

That's Scarborough. And I'll always be grateful for the confidence it gave me, the high standard it sets and the fellow student I did eventually manage to bed there.

Lucy Prebble

to suggest that they knew it was all futile. They would frequently break off from the routines to dust themselves with talcum powder, while blocks of stage gore in the lighting rig gradually thawed, to rain blood over the stage. The overall effect, of a cabaret collapsing at the end of the world, was devastating.

There was also the first production at the Festival of a play by Sarah Kane who, since her death in 1999, had become one of the playwrights most frequently chosen by students for entries to the Festival – an almost patron saint figure for many drama students. That said, Oxford University's production of Crave was anything but reverential, taking the four static voices of Kane's oblique text and setting them within a framework of movement, which described the routines of everyday life and clearly delineated the possible relationships between them.

Above: Ramesh Meyyappan in *Mistero Buffo*

Left: *Mrs Blackwell Eats Her Cake*

If Longwave and Crave both echoed post-9/11 anxieties, then Edinburgh University's Mrs Blackwell Eats Her Cake spoke to the newly politicised generation of students, offering a satirical mirror image of the Thatcher years, in the politicking of a school staff room. Equally successful – if more modishly apolitical – was another new play: Sheffield University's Liquid, written by Lucy Prebble and filled with many of the excellent one-liners which characterised The Sugar Syndrome: her first play at the Royal Court only a year and a half later.

The Festival also saw a new adaptation of Notes from Underground. Not the Dostoyevsky story that had launched Buzz Goodbody's career in 1967, but Eric Bogosian's nightmarish, fragmented tale of a social misfit who abducts two children. Appropriately enough, this new Notes From Underground was awarded the Buzz Goodbody Award. Continuing in this vein of dislocation was the Sunday Times New Play Award winner: Tom Green's Muswell Hill – a pair of intercut monologues delivered in a false perspective set, which gradually unfolded a tale of paranoia, casual violence and cannibalism.

It wasn't all politics, fragmentation and post-apocalyptic misery, though. Nottingham University offered light relief in the form of The Hush, a frantically paced, devised homage to the silent films of Charlie Chaplin and Buster

Keaton. The show was a huge hit and was awarded the new 'Festgoer's Award' – an innovation by Nick Stimson: the award was decided by a vote to recognise the most popular show of the Festival.

Also on show was the sublime work of deaf performer Ramesh Meyyappan's Mistero Buffo / A Woman Alone. This was elegantly summarised by Dan Bye in one of the reviews which won him his second Harold Hobson Student Theatre Critic prize: 'Ramesh Meyyappan is an extraordinary physical performer, with control, versatility and charm… [he] has taken Dario Fo's text about a buffoonish drunk and removed the text. It's an extraordinary achievement; it leaves one wondering why Fo needed words in the first place.'

2002 also saw the end of Ian Shuttleworth's astonishing 12-year stint as editor of Noises Off. When he took over from Stephen Jeffreys in 1991 the magazine had just switched from manual typewriters to electric, and was laid out using cow gum and Blu-Tack. The operation which he passed on to Andrew Haydon and Rachel Smyth had a working network of around 15 computers, bespoke software courtesy of longstanding Noises Off staff member Ben Curthoys, and on-screen layout processes.

Beyond the march of technology, there is the inestimable care that he took nurturing the magazine, its staff and its writers. His passionate and rigorous defence of theatre criticism's purpose was continually an inspiration to those writing for Noises Off, and also gave pause for thought to

The Hush

many an affronted young actor who would storm into the Vitadome searching for a young critic who had damned a show. A while later, the same actor would often be seen deep in conversation with Ian, nodding earnestly about that critic's right to their viewpoint, no matter how much they might wish to dispute it.

Festival Director Nick Stimson remembers:

One of the central bodies of the NSDF is Noises Off. The aspect of Festival that won me over when I was first thinking of applying for the job was the tremendous work carried out by the Magazine. It was a little like having a hungry tiger on a very thin chain prowling around. Fantastic irreverent reviews. No holds barred. Just what it should be.

2003

Nick Stimson's third and final Festival as Artistic Director saw his efforts of the past three years rewarded by one of the most impressive Festivals of recent times. Even the weather was substantially better than normal. Elsewhere, there was also a sense that British Theatre was being reinvigorated, with Nicolas Hytner recently appointed Artistic Director of the National Theatre, and 1975 NSDF award winner Michael Boyd the RSC. Interviews with both were featured in the week's first issue of Noises Off.

The artistic standards on show over the course of the week were remarkable. The Festival opened with an impressive revival of Ariane Mnouchkine's 1789 performed by 30 pupils of St Paul's Girls School directed by 16-year-old Imogen Walford. There was the first production of a Shakespeare play since 1996, ably performed by a cast of LIPA graduates. Graduates of the Lecoq School offered a characteristically polished clown show, while a 15-minute sketch from Liverpool Hope University called The Dudleys featured a startling combination of arrestingly foul-mouthed comedy and assured physical theatre.

However, even in a year of the highest quality, there were four very disparate pieces which stood out: The Freudian Slip – a brilliantly witty comic play from Exeter University; Dartington College's intelligent and sensuous devised piece See You Swoon; and Edinburgh University's production of Chris Perkin's Sunday Times Student Playwright Award-winning new play Like Skinnydipping, a masterfully constructed tale of adolescent pain and returning to one's roots set over the course of seven years, which boasted a large cast, and a healthy disregard for realism. But it was Cambridge University's brilliant realisation of Enda Walsh's Bedbound that carried off virtually every other major award of the Festival. 2003's Harold Hobson prize-winner Ed Lake, summarises it perfectly:

See You Swoon by Dartington College

Photograph © Allan Titmuss

Photograph © Allan Titmuss

Above left: Edinburgh University's *Like Skinnydipping*

Above: Cambridge University's *Bedbound*

The level of performative focus evident here far exceeds anything I've seen at this or any NSDF, not to mention anything else on the amateur or professional stage. I know these people, and I know they're quite mad anyway. Even so, it comes as a bit of a shock to find that from the audience Khalid Abdalla looks like about eighty feet of psychotic volcano and Cressida Trew like a magically articulate fishing lure... I think this Bedbound is splendid, and if I'd made it I'd be strutting like the uncrowned king of Am Dram I was.

The week closed with a new show that had been collaboratively devised over the course of the Festival, which culminated in a spectacular pyrotechnic display outside the Spa centre. The Festival even had its first fringe event for over a decade in the form of a girl sitting sealed for long periods of time in an unfeasibly small box situated in the Spa Centre's Reception.

I was always struck by just how much the professional theatre world could learn from the NSDF. If it encouraged the same spirit of openness and honesty, our theatre would be a far healthier place.

Nick Stimson

2004

After three hard years, Nick Stimson had decided not to renew his contract as Artistic Director. He felt that the Festival had taken him too far away from writing and directing and wanted to get back. In his three brief years he had effected the remarkable transformation of the Festival, from the cottage industry run from a loft in Muswell Hill into a professionally run arts organisation, thereby ensuring its continuation.

Nick's replacement, appointed shortly after the 2003 Festival, was Andrew Loretto, a graduate of Glasgow University and Royal Welsh College of Music and Drama, who had worked for the Sherman Theatre, Cardiff, and was Artistic Director of Theatre in the Mill, Bradford. As a director and writer Andrew had staged many diverse pieces of work around the UK, which fused text, visuals, movement and sound to create highly energised theatre. He was an ideal candidate to keep the Festival moving forward, and the Board leapt at the opportunity.

NSDF04 brought a new team of selectors and visiting artists to the Festival – many attending for the first time. New ideas were piloted, always with the spirit of endeavour

By the end of my time with the NSDF I felt we were on course. We had built a strong funding base that gave the NSDF some security for the future. The Festivals were attracting record numbers of participants and record entries of productions.

Perhaps the most important aspect of my time at the NSDF was taking hold of the baton handed on by Clive and not dropping it. That much I hope I did.

Something I want to record is that all of this was a team effort. Rachel Williams and later, Ian Abbott, were instrumental and vital in this work and I thank them and acknowledge their immense contribution. Huge thanks are also due to the excellent people on the selection team, NOFF, and those other key figures who are the NSDF. And there's another, unsung group who deserve massive thanks: the NSDF Board: Robert Hewison, Glen Walford, Timothy West, Stephen Jeffreys, Donna Munday and in particular, Barbara Matthews. They were tireless in defending the meaning of the NSDF. I would also like to record the importance and central role I tried to foster for the admirable Tech Team. One of my aims was to present a Festival that recognised the totality of theatre: writers, actors, producers, directors, technical crews, design, critics and organisational staff.

Nick Stimson

Photograph © Allan Titmuss

Above: Peterborough College's *As If A Rag*

Right: Hull University's *Tapped*

Photograph © Allan Titmuss

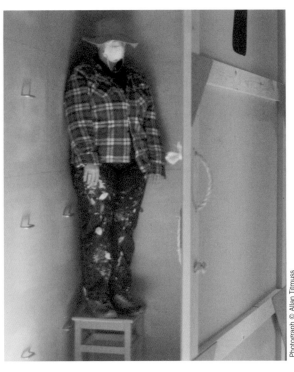

Above: Fiona Clift in Reigate Grammar School's *Greek*
Right: Hull University's *Unlucky For Some*

and the right to fail that is central to the ethos of the Festival. One such event as part of the new line-up is The Parting Shots, finishing the Festival with a showcase of work to emerge from the workshop programme.

Andrew Loretto

The work on show at the Festival also seemed to chime in with this ongoing spirit of experimentation. Hull University Scarborough Campus' theatre studies department presented their most original offering yet – Unlucky For Some – an installation piece in which audience members took individual routes through a selection of 13 crates, each containing a different performance, including an S&M Macbeth, an audition for The Blair Witch Project, and a girl dressed as a Squirrel 'doing' Jack Nicholson in The Shining. Also devised was Peterborough College's unexpectedly moving As If A Rag – two soldiers in a rubbish-strewn pit, shown dying over the course of fifteen minutes in some unspecified apocalypse. This was paired with Hull University's poetic Tapped – two naked lovers in a bath filled with tiny polystyrene balls, rhapsodising for fifteen minutes.

Seventeen-year-old Fiona Clift from Reigate Grammar school was awarded the Buzz Goodbody Award for her

direction of Steven Berkoff's Greek, performed by a four-strong all-female cast, including Clift herself, which revelled in the obscenity of Berkoff's narrative. The Festival also saw the welcome return of Iain Ormsby-Knox, directing students from the Liverpool Institute of Performing Arts in a flawless production of Jonathan Harvey's Beautiful Thing and, in a Festival that saw the plays entered divide mainly into extant texts and devised pieces, a new tragi-comic play by Tiffany Wood and Charlotte Riley called Shaking Cecelia, which won the Sunday Times Playwriting Award.

Also impressive was Queens University, Belfast's The Laramie Project – a piece of verbatim 'docu-theatre' – originally created by an American company, following the murder of gay student Matthew Shepherd in Laramie, Wyoming, 1998; it was re-imagined by the Northern Irish company to take on meanings beyond its immediate subject, to create a thoughtful comment on violence. Its director Des Kennedy was awarded the Bush Theatre Director's Bursary.

One of the greatest artistic successes of the Festival was provided by the invited production, which came as part of the Festival's new participation in the International Theatre Schools conference: Political Assassinator [sic] – a 40-minute dance-based exploration of the Israeli-Palestinian conflict, performed by Israeli Yoram Mosenzon.

2005

NSDF in the 21st Century is facing up to the challenges of its role as a national resource in a landscape where young people's theatre provision is becoming more inclusive and reflective of our diverse and changing society. NSDF now offers national outreach workshops in collaboration with student theatre groups, colleges and universities. These workshops raise awareness of the Festival and encourage students from currently under-represented groups to think about attending or entering productions.

NSDF is also now looking beyond the UK for its regular collaborative partners. NSDF should stimulate future theatre-makers to think on a global basis and to work collaboratively. Following a pilot exchange programme in 2004, NSDF05 will showcase a range of visiting international student performances as well as offering touring opportunities to UK students. NSDF continues to be a unique national resource, straddling the journey from post-GCSE up to emerging artist. NSDF will continue to evolve, embracing new venues, working methods and artistic forms. Ultimately it is the students' Festival and as such we should be able to respond to their artistic concerns, needs and aspirations in the future.

Andrew Loretto

The Festival has always proved that it is endlessly capable of reinventing itself: the moments when it has looked nearest to disaster have always been those when it has made its boldest choices. Whatever challenges and changes it faces in the coming years, it is certain that what will remain unchanged is that at its core will always be a passion for theatre that has kept the Festival alive for fifty years, and will keep it alive for fifty more.

No event as vast as the NSDF lasts fifty years without a legion of immeasurably talented and dedicated people being involved. There have been many for whom space has not been available in sufficient quantities to do them justice. Their input is acknowledged through the Festival Director's Awards, given to a small sample of such people as have given the Festival outstanding service unmarked elsewhere. Pride of place goes to the inaugural six honoured by Clive: Lon David, Stephen Jeffreys, Steve Garrett, Steven Downs,

Nick Kraven and Iain Ormsby-Knox , who, for several years, gave all his spare time and more to the NSDF as a front line selector, selection administrator, giving workshops and organising them, revolutionising a complex ticket system for all, and generally proving a brilliant problem solver.

That could apply equally well to scores of technicians, those geniuses who have transformed even dead areas into practical, even attractive, theatres, which they have then manned before, quite often, executing a swift turnaround possibly involving totally changing the theatre's shape overnight. All of which, and more, is represented by FD Awards to just two of the past Technical masterminds: Steve Garrett and Nick Kraven.

Much the same spirit and dedication has usually been shown by the teams of Local Organisers, some of whom, like the more experienced Techies, can later be found running or servicing theatres, whether, for example, as the youngest Chief Executive ever of the Everyman, Cheltenham (Bubble Lodge, now a producer); Rosemary Squire (now Chief Executive of the large Ambassadors Theatre Group); Award-winning sound designer Paul Arditti; or Patrick Murphy (now Lloyd-Webber's Really Useful Theatre Company Productions Manager). The motley crew producing Noises Off night after sleepless night do an incredible job in catching the shifting themes and moods of the living kaleidoscope of talents and experiences of the Festival – every year.

Thanks are also due to the succession of highly engaging discussion chairs of recent years including the wonderfully entertaining (though occasionally incomprehensible) actor and writer Shaun Prendergast, the endearing stage and TV actor Ben Miller (of Armstrong & Miller fame) and, since 2001, the suave, cool, authoritative stage, film and TV actor Mark Bowden.

All three, like most of the professionals taking workshops, giving talks or helping the Tech Team and Noises Off were, until 2001, themselves past-participants at the NSDF when students, which has helped both continuity and the undeniable Festival spirit of camaraderie. That spirit perhaps explains the bond felt by the majority of those going on into the theatrical professions, even with those whose NSDF experiences were in different years.

The Festival's indebtedness to The Sunday Times for its fifty years of unbroken support is enormous, and we pay tribute, to those staff members most involved, including the visionary pioneers, sadly no longer with us (Sir Harold Hobson, Kenneth Pearson and Jack Lambert) and the many Editors and Arts Editors, including the particularly supportive Harold Evans and lately David Mills and Helen Hawkins. They have done student drama and the world of theatre an outstanding service.

APPENDIX

All shows, whether selected or invited, presented at the National Student Drama Festival are listed by year. Some self-selecting Fringe shows, less well documented, are omitted. Unattributed awards (the majority) were given by the Festival judges and are shown in brackets after the relevant show's credits, together with any prescribed awards. Any awards not related to a specific show are listed, with each year's sponsors (sp) and, where known, the names of the local organisers (lo) and technical directors (td) at the end of that year's lists.

(a) = award/s; (n) = new; (ns) = new student writing; (tr) = translated by; (ad) = adapted; (d) = devised by the company. All marked as (ad) or (d) are new, unless otherwise specified. As precise records of some translations are sketchy, new ones are so designated only where there is certainty; (ns tr) = confirmed new translation by students. Not all translators are credited, but unmarked translations are usually the well-established versions.

ISPC is the International Student Playwriting Competition winner, usually given a rehearsed reading at the NSDF, but never performed there.

(nc) = non-competitor; mostly invited or guest shows, including all from abroad.

Chris Barlas' *The Private Life of Superman*, from the University of Bradford, 1977

1956

The Broken Heart by John Ford, Heywood Society, Peterhouse College, Cambridge

Macbeth by William Shakespeare, London School of Economics Dramatic Society (nc)

Macbeth by William Shakespeare, UCW Aberystwyth Dramatic Society

Our Town by Thornton Wilder, Student Players, Regent Street Polytechnic (a: *Sunday Times* Drama Trophy)

Tonight We Improvise by Luigi Pirandello (tr Frederick May), Leeds University Union Theatre Group

sp: *The Sunday Times*

1957

Huis Clos by Jean-Paul Sartre, Dramatic Society, University College, London (nc)

Investigation by Ugo Betti (ns tr J W James & J P Scott), Bristol University Dramatic Society

Richard II by William Shakespeare, Cardiff University Players

Tiger at the Gates by Jean Giraudoux, Dramatic Society, Queen's University, Belfast (a: *Sunday Times* Drama Trophy)

Home of the Brave by Arthur Laurents, American Student Drama Group (nc)

The Maker of Dreams by Oliphant Down, Students' Union Drama Group, Acton Technical College (nc)

The Silver Curlew by Eleanor Farjeon, RADA (nc)

sp: *The Sunday Times*

1958

The Crucible by Arthur Miller, Dramatic Society, University College, Aberystwyth

The Marriage of Figaro by Pierre Beaumarchais (ns tr J W James), Bristol University Dramatic Society

Nightmare Abbey (n) by Anthony Sharp (ad from Thomas Love Peacock), Dramatic Club, Balliol College, Oxford

The Shepherd's Chameleon by Eugène Ionesco (tr Sasha Moorsom), Dramatic Society, New College, Oxford (nc)

The Skin of Our Teeth by Thornton Wilder, Dramatic Society, University College, London

A Sleep of Prisoners by Christopher Fry, University College Cardiff Players (a: *Sunday Times* Drama Trophy)

The Room (n) by Harold Pinter, University Drama Department & Bristol Old Vic Theatre School (nc)

sp: *The Sunday Times*; lo: Brian Ives; td: David Machin

1959

Crime Passionnel by Jean-Paul Sartre, English Dramatic Society, University College, Bangor

The Crucifixion (ns) by Michael Kustow, Dramatic Society, Wadham College, Oxford (nc)

Downstairs (ns) by Caryl Churchill, Dramatic Society, Oriel College, Oxford (nc)

The Good Woman of Szechuan by Bertolt Brecht, Hull University Dramatic Society

He Who Gets Slapped by Leonid Andreyev (tr Leonard Ingold), Leeds University Theatre Group

Six Characters in Search of an Author by Luigi Pirandello (tr Frederick May), Guild Theatre Group, Birmingham University (a: *Sunday Times* Drama Trophy)

The Swamp Dwellers (n) by Wole Soyinka, Nigerian Drama Group (nc)

Variations by Aleksandar Obrenovic, Academic Theatre of Belgrade University (nc)

sp: *The Sunday Times*; lo: Clive Wolfe

1960

The Bald Prima Donna by Eugène Ionesco, Apollo Society, St Catherine's College, Oxford (nc)

The Beauty from Samos by Menander (ns tr Joanna Richardson & Patric Dickenson), Sheffield University Student Drama Group (nc)

Coriolanus by William Shakespeare, University of Nottingham Dramatic Society

The Duchess of Malfi by John Webster, Guild Theatre Group, Birmingham University

A Full Moon in March by W B Yeats, Dramatic Society, Stranmillis Training College, Belfast (nc)

Hamlet by William Shakespeare, Dramatic Society, University College, London

The Hole by N F Simpson, Eglesfield Players, Queen's College, Oxford (nc)

Jacques by Eugène Ionesco, Experimental Theatre Club, Oxford University (nc)

The Kitchen by Arnold Wesker, Cambridge University Mummers (nc)

Picnic en Campagne by Fernando Arrabal (tr David Britt & Brian Blumfield), Cambridge University Mummers (nc)

The Sport of My Mad Mother by Ann Jellicoe, Durham Colleges Dramatic Society (a: *Sunday Times* Drama Trophy)

Sweeney Agonistes by T S Eliot, Hull University Dramatic Society (nc)

The Circus Tralabomba (revue), Poland (nc)

sp: *The Sunday Times*; lo: Andrew Hyslop

1961

From 1961 onwards, short plays competed, for the NUS Plaque.

Auto-da-fe by Tennessee Williams, Guild Theatre Group, Birmingham University

Cats of Egypt by T B Morris, Nottinghamshire County Training College Dramatic Society

The Dice (n) by Forbes Bramble, London University Drama Society

The Great God Brown by Eugene O'Neill, Guild Theatre Group, Birmingham University

A Kind of Nothing (ns) by Bill Morrison, Queen's University Belfast Dramatic Society

The Lower Depths by Maxim Gorky, University College London Dramatic Society

A Man Named John (ns) by Keith Miles, University Players Dramatic Society, University College, Oxford

A Penny for a Song by John Whiting, University of Bristol Dramatic Society

The Proposal by Anton Chekhov, Guild Theatre Group, Birmingham University

Serjeant Musgrave's Dance by John Arden, Union Theatre Group, Leeds University (a: *Sunday Times* Drama Trophy)

Their Souls in Hell (n) by Gerard Galloway, Hull University Dramatic Society

Waiting for Godot by Samuel Beckett, Liverpool University Dramatic Society

The Zoo Story by Edward Albee, The Shirley Society, St Catharine's College, Cambridge (a: NUS One-Act Plaque)

sp: *The Sunday Times*; lo: Brian MacArthur

1962

Antigone by Christopher Logue, London School of Economics Drama Society

The Bald Prima Donna by Eugène Ionesco, Dublin University Players

The Birthday Party by Harold Pinter, Union Drama Club, Manchester University

Camino Real by Tennessee Williams, Bristol University Dramatic Society (a: *Sunday Times* Drama Trophy)

Draw the Fires by Ernst Toller (tr Edward Crankshaw), Leeds University Union Theatre Group

El Deleitoso by Lope de Rueda and **El Rey** by Ghelderode and mime, University of Madrid (nc)

The Dumb Waiter by Harold Pinter, Edinburgh University Dramatic Society

Henry IV by Luigi Pirandello (tr Frederick May), Liverpool University Dramatic Society

The Post Office by Rabindranath Tagore, Guild Theatre Group, Birmingham University

Three Actors and their Drama by Michel de Ghelderode (tr G Hauger), Leeds University Union Theatre Group

The View from Poppa's Head (n) by Gwyn A Williams, Dramatic Society, University College, Aberystwyth (a: NUS One-Act Plaque)

Woyzeck by Georg Buchner (tr John Holmstrom), Dramatic Society, University College, London

sp: *The Sunday Times*; lo: Anthony Cole

1963

The Anniversary by Anton Chekhov, Trent Park Dramatic Society

Brand by Henrik Ibsen, Liverpool University Dramatic Society (a: *Sunday Times* Drama Trophy)

The Caucasian Chalk Circle by Bertolt Brecht, Edinburgh University Dramatic Society

The Fire Raisers by Max Frisch, Dublin University Players

The Hole by N F Simpson, Everyman Club, Nottingham University

The Killer by Eugène Ionesco, Guild Theatre Group, Birmingham University

The Lesson by Eugène Ionesco, Oxford University Dramatic Society

The Link by August Strindberg, Loughborough Colleges Dramatic Society

The Maids by Jean Genet, Keele University Drama Group (a: NUS One-Act Plaque)

The Sandbox by Edward Albee, Mermaid Dramatic Society, St Andrews University

A Slight Ache by Harold Pinter, Bristol University Dramatic Society

Volpone by Ben Jonson, Southampton University Theatre Group

The Sport of My Mad Mother by Ann Jellicoe, Little Theatre, University of Cape Town (nc)

sp: *The Sunday Times*; lo: Dick Lord

1964

The Chairs by Eugène Ionesco, Dramatic Society, St Luke's, Exeter (a: NUS One-Act Plaque)

The Chairs by Eugène Ionesco, Aberystwyth University

Dr Maccabre by Jocelyn Powell, Southampton University Theatre Group

Fando and Lis by Fernando Arrabal, Leeds University Union Theatre Group

Lord Halewyn by Michel de Ghelderode, Sussex University Theatre

Kiyotsune by Zeami Motokiyo, Nottingham University Dramatic Society

Measure for Measure by William Shakespeare, Durham University Dramatic Society

Mind the Flowers by Eugène Ionesco, Liverpool University Dramatic Society

Rhinoceros by Eugène Ionesco, University Players, Oxford University

Six Characters in Search of an Author by Luigi Pirandello, University of Bristol Dramatic Society

Three Sisters by Anton Chekhov, Leeds University Union Theatre Group (a: *Sunday Times* Drama Trophy)

Under Milk Wood by Dylan Thomas, Nottingham Everyman Society, Nottingham University

Uncle Maroje and the Others by Marin Drzic, The Theatre Academy of Bratislava (nc)

sp: *The Sunday Times*; lo: Peter Walton

1965

Black and White (dance to music by Bartók), Dramatic Society, St Mary's, Newcastle

The Collection by Harold Pinter, Newton Park Training College, Bath (a: NUS One-Act Plaque)

The Crucible by Arthur Miller, University of Manchester Drama Group (a: *Sunday Times* Drama Trophy)

The Dumb Waiter by Harold Pinter, Dramatic Society, St Mary's, Twickenham

In Camera by Jean-Paul Sartre (tr Stuart Gilbert), Keele University Drama Group

Judith by Jean Giraudoux, Dramatic Society, University College, London

Live Like Pigs by John Arden, Cardiff University Players

Mrs Evergreen (group improvisation), Weymouth Training College Drama Society

Next Time I'll Sing to You by James Saunders, Durham University Theatre

Out of the Flying Pan by David Campton, Theatre Group, University College, Aberystwyth

The Public Eye by Peter Shaffer, Nottingham University Dramatic Society

Pullman Car Hiawatha by Thornton Wilder, Hendon College of Technology Dramatic Society

The Soldier's Tale by C F Ramuz with music by Igor Stravinsky, Leeds University Union Theatre Group

The Visit by Friedrich Durrenmatt, Guild Theatre Group, Birmingham University

The Zoo Story by Edward Albee, Leicester University Drama Society

The Playboy of the Western World by J M Synge, The Bucharest Student House of Culture Ensemble (nc)

sp: *The Sunday Times*; lo: Andy Rushbridge

1966

Act Without Words* by Samuel Beckett, Guild Theatre Group, Birmingham University

The American Dream by Edward Albee, Durham University Theatre Group

A Bitter Taste (dramatised poems by World War One fighters), Drama Society, St Peter's College, Saltley

Caligula* by Albert Camus, Southampton University Theatre Group (a: *Sunday Times* Drama Trophy)

Cécile by Jean Anouilh, Liverpool University Dramatic Society

Comedy, Satire, Irony and Deeper Meaning by Christian Dietrich-Grabbe (tr Barbara Wright), Manchester University Drama Group

The Country Wife by William Wycherley, Dublin University Players

Creditors by August Strindberg, Manchester University Drama Group

The Duchess of Malfi by John Webster, Leeds University Union Theatre Group

The Dumb Waiter by Harold Pinter, Lancaster University Theatre Group

Endgame* by Samuel Beckett, Keele University Drama Group (a: NUS One-Act Plaque)

The Fire Raisers by Max Frisch, Bristol University Dramatic Society

The Trials of Brother Jero by Wole Soyinka, Bradford Institute of Technology Drama Group

Plutos by Aristophanes, New Stage Group, Goethe University, Frankfurt (nc)

sp: *The Sunday Times*; lo: John Strauss

* Presented at St Martin's Theatre, London, 10–16 January 1966 by producer Peter Bridge

1967

The Bear by Anton Chekhov, Sheffield University Theatre Group

The Caretaker by Harold Pinter, York University Drama Society

The Chinese Wall† by Max Frisch, Leeds University Union Theatre Group (a: *Sunday Times* Drama Trophy)

Danton's Death by Georg Buchner, Durham University Theatre Group

Galileo by Bertolt Brecht, Guild Theatre Group, Birmingham University

The Hole by N F Simpson, Leeds University Union Theatre Group

Jacques by Eugène Ionesco, Manchester University Drama Group

Jenousia† by Rene de Obaldia, Experimental Theatre Club, Oxford University (a: NUS One-Act Plaque)

John Thomas by Charles Wood, Lancaster University Drama Society

Notes from Underground† (ad from Dostoievsky & dir by Buzz Goodbody), University of Sussex Theatre

The Only Jealousy of Emer by W B Yeats, University of East Anglia Drama Society

A Resounding Tinkle by N F Simpson, Players, University College, Cardiff

Six Over the Severn (an 'intimate revue') by Jeremy Treglown, Dramatic Society, St Peter's College, Saltley

Spare† by Charles Wood, Guild Theatre Group, Birmingham University

Swan Song by Anton Chekhov, Dramatic Society, St Mary's, Twickenham

sp: *The Sunday Times*; lo: Allan Jones

† Presented at the Garrick Theatre, London, 23–29 January 1967 by Peter Bridge

1968

Fando and Lis by Fernando Arrabal, Sheffield University Theatre Group

The Homecoming by Harold Pinter, Edinburgh University Drama Society (a: *Sunday Times* Drama Trophy)

Liberation Day (n) by John R Rudlin, Dramatic Society, Rolle College, Exmouth

Lysistrata by Aristophanes, Hendon College of Technology Dramatic Society

Marat/Sade by Peter Weiss, Dramatic Society, University College, Bangor

Mother Courage by Bertolt Brecht, Leeds University Union Theatre Group

The Rehearsal by Jean Anouilh, Bristol University Dramatic Society

The Room by Harold Pinter, Student Union Dramatic Society, Brighton University (a: NUS One-Act Plaque)

The Shepherd's Chameleon by Eugène Ionesco, City of Liverpool College of Education Dramatic Society

Tatenberg II by Armand Gatti, Liverpool University Dramatic Society

The Two Executioners by Fernando Arrabal, Enfield College of Technology Entertainments Society

Waiting for Godot by Samuel Beckett, Guild Theatre Group, Birmingham University

sp: *The Sunday Times*; lo:Peter O'Neill

1969

The Amazing Harold Show (ns) by Patrick Fletcher, Brighton College of Art (nc)

Broche (n) by Stewart Conn, Edinburgh University Dramatic Society

Chronicles of Hell by Michel de Ghelderode, Keele University Drama Group

Clearway by Vivienne C Welburn, Nottingham University Dramatic Society

Cyclops by Euripides (tr Percy Bysshe Shelley), Durham University Theatre

The Death of Doctor Faust by Michel de Ghelderode, Leicester College of Art & Technology Theatre Group

The Dynamic Death-Defying Leap of Timothy Satupon the Great (n) by Peter Hawkins, Newcastle University Drama Society

How Ho Ho Rose and Fell by Michael Weller, Union Drama Group, Manchester University

I Am Not the Eiffel Tower by Ecaterina Oproiu (tr Adrienne Burgess), Bristol University Dramatic Society

Krapp's Last Tape by Samuel Beckett, Dryden Society, Trinity College, Cambridge (a: NUS One-Act Plaque)

Metamorphosis (n) by John Abulafia, Federation of Brighton Students

Mexican (n) by David Pammenter, Dramatic Society, St Luke's, Exeter

No Fixed Abode by Clive Exton, The Waifs, Dundee University

Raw (d), Dramatic Society, Rolle College, Exmouth, Judges' Personal Award

Where Are You Going, Hollis Jay? by Benjamin Bradford, University of Kent, Canterbury

X (ns) by Pam Aubrey, Essex University Theatre Arts Society

Zoo Zoo Widdershins Zoo (n) by Kevin Laffan, Leicester University (a: *Sunday Times* Drama Trophy; Allied Theatre Productions Award)

sp: *The Sunday Times*; lo: Mike Hall; td: Ian Cowan

1970

Aggression (ns) by Shell Abulafia, Institute of Education, London, Drama Society

The Ancient Mariner (ns) by Andrew Wistreich with music by Stuart Jones, Actors' Workshop, York University (a: *Sunday Times* Drama Trophy)

Doors (n) by Richard Drain, Nottingham University Dramatic Society

Flight (n) by Gordon Roberts, Edinburgh University Dramatic Society

From Out of a Box (n) by George MacEwan Green, Leicester University Theatre (a: NUS One-Act Plaque)

The Golden Thread (n) by Kevin West & Michael Milford, Leicester Polytechnic

Hamlet with Four Princes (ad from Shakespeare), University College, Cardiff (nc)

The Hole (group improvisation), The Group Travelling Company

Looking Forward to 1942 (revue), Bradford College of Art (nc)

Madly Madly (n) by Peter Hawkins, Durham University

Peribañez by Lope de Vega (tr John Brotherton), Guild Theatre Group, Birmingham University

Placings (ns) by Chris MacGregor, University of East Anglia Drama Society

Saint Rosa I Die (ns) by David Porter, New College of Speech & Drama, London

Sleep to Wake (n) by Cheryl Greenaway, Exeter University Drama Society

The Stronghold (ns) by Rod Lewis, Sussex University Theatre Club

Time Exposure by David Compton, Newcastle University Dramatic Society

Viet Rock by Megan Terry, Keele University Drama Group

sp: *The Sunday Times*; lo: Peter Kilgour

1971

Before and After (ns) by David Farrall (based on *The Seagull* by Anton Chekhov), The Waifs, Dundee University

Charles the Martyr (n) by Snoo Wilson, University of East Anglia Drama Society

Comus by John Milton (ad by Martin Pennock), Buckland Players, University Hall, Berkshire

Grass (n) co-ordinated by Andrew Wistreich, Grass Roots, York University

The Junior Bleeders (n) by James Robson, Bretton Hall Drama Society

King Herod Explains (n) by Conor Cruise O'Brien, Edinburgh University Drama Society

The Mirror and the Star (n) by Paul Swain, St Bartholomew's Hospital Medical School Drama Society (a: Albion Productions Award)

Paradise Lost (ad from Milton), Keele Drama Group

The Party by Slawomir Mrozek (tr Nicholas Benthell), Southampton University Theatre Group

Tommy by Graham Devlin (ad from the music of The Who), Experimental Theatre Company, Oxford University

The Tragical History of Dr Faustus (ad from Marlowe), I M Marsh College of Physical Education

Xerxes by Andre Benedetto, University of Essex Theatre Arts Society

John Ford's Cuban Missile Crisis (n) by Albert Hunt, The Welfare State (nc)

Dr Strangebrew's Plastic Hand, (n) The Welfare State (nc)

Offending the Audience by Peter Handke, The Other Company (nc)

Superman by Pip Simmons and the group, The Pip Simmons Theatre Group (nc)

Sunday Times Playwriting Award, Gabriel Josipovici, Evidence of Intimacy

sp: The Sunday Times; lo: Vicki Goodwin

1972

The Audition (n) by Donald Nunes, West Midlands College of Education

Bromius! Evohe! (ad from The Bacchae by Euripides), Bingley College of Education

The Crucifiction of Black Antag (n) by Dedwydd Jones, Cardiff University

Interred Side by Side (n, inspired by The Phantom Tollbooth by Norton Juster), Dramatic Society, Rolle College, Exmouth

MacRune's Guevara by John Spurling, UP, Manchester University Drama Department Postgraduates & Granada Bursary Students of Manchester Polytechnic Theatre School

The Marshall McLuhan Foodshow (d), Intergalactic Space Corps, Keele University Drama Group

Prometheus Rebound (n) by Nigel Dottridge & Ken Montague, Essex University Theatre Arts Society

The Syracuse Myth (ns) by George Blackledge, Barts Drama, St Bartholomew's Hospital Medical School

Woyzeck by Georg Buchner, Northern Counties College of Education

The Moshe Dayan Extravaganza by Michael Almaz, The General Will (nc)

The Rupert Show (n) by David Edgar, The General Will (nc)

The National Interest (n) by David Edgar, The General Will (nc)

A Christmas Naming Ceremony, The Welfare State (nc)

Fallacy (d), Keele Performance Group

James Harold Wilson Sinks the Bismarck (ns) by the group, Bradford Art College

The Destruction of Dresden ('a carnival for Valentine's eve') (n), Bradford Art College

The Barrow Boys by Jeff Nuttall, Mr Spooner's Magic Theatre

Sunday Times Playwriting Award, Mike Lawrence The Ivory Cell

sp: The Sunday Times; lo: Ken Westgate

1973

After Liverpool by James Saunders, London University Drama Society

The Cross Buttock Show by Henry Livings, Leicester Polytechnic Theatre Group

Dearth (n) by Gray Green, Leeds University Union Theatre Group

Decent Things (n) by Richard Crane, Bradford University Drama Group

Fando and Lis by Fernando Arrabal, UKC Dramatics, Kent University

Lear (n, ad from King Lear by William Shakespeare), York University Drama Society

Man in the Moon and Footsteps on Other Faces (n) by Henry Ehrlich, Southampton University Theatre Group

Medea by Euripides, Drama Department, Neville's Cross College, Durham

Next Time I'll Sing to You by James Saunders, Drama Studio, London

Oedipus by Ted Hughes (ad from Seneca), Durham University Theatre

An Off-White Comedy (n) by Jan Domm (ad from Piet Niemand), Newcastle University Dramatic Society

Pictures (d), Theatre Workshop, University College, Bangor

Puppet (d) by Harry Cayton, Manticore Mime, Durham University

Rosencrantz and Guildenstern are Dead by Tom Stoppard, Leeds University Union Theatre Group

The Short List (n) by Donald Nunes, Students Union, West Midland College of Education

Tedderella (n) by David Edgar, Bradford University Drama Group

The Unnerving Castration of Conformist Adolescents (ns) by Dave McCann, Dirty Wellington Boot on the Roof Revue Company, Aston University (nc)

In One Breath by Lech Raczak & Ewa Wojciak (based on the work of Stanislaw Brananczak), Theatre of the 8th Day, Poznan, Poland (nc)

Positively the Last Appearance of Ted Bijou This Side of the Trent (d, n), Filey Hippodrome Theatre Company, York University Graduates

Blindfold (n, work in progress), RAT Theatre, Keele University Graduates

Sunday Times Playwriting Award: Tina Brown, Under the Bamboo Tree

Michael Codron Award: Shoestring Theatre, York University, Life in a Chocolate Factory

sp: The Sunday Times; lo: Charles Bishop

1974

Alice Through the Looking Glass by Rob Robertson & Ben Timmis (ad from Lewis Carroll), St Bartholomew's Hospital Medical School Drama Society

Blue Plastic Yolk (ns) by Nicholas Blane, Hockerill College of Education, Bishop Stortford

Boxes (ns) by Pip Royall, Students' Union, New College of Speech & Drama (a: Michael Codron Award, Pip Royall)

Cupid's Happy Heart Show (d), Café Theatre, Warwick University

Diolch am Bopeth by Angela Williams (ns, tr Wyn Bowen-Harries), University College, Aberystwyth also played in English as Thank You, Jane for Everything

The Foursome by E A Whitehead, Newcastle University Drama Society

The Importance of Being Earnest by Oscar Wilde, City of Leicester College of Education

Liberated Zone by David Edgar (ns, ad from an improvisation), Bingley College of Education Drama Department

The Marowitz Hamlet by Charles Marowitz, Durham University Theatre

The Other Judas (ns) by Rob Robertson, St Bartholomew's Hospital Medical School Drama Society

Pantoloons by Mike Gatti (n, ad from Richard Humphry & Peter Johnson), Stage, Loughborough University

Papadopoulos Rex (n, d), Shoestring Theatre, York University

Portrait of My Ladies (n) by Frances Sacker, Students Union, New College of Speech & Drama

Thank You, Jane, for Everything by Angela Williams, University College, Aberystwyth also played in Welsh as Diolch am Bopeth

Three Women by Sylvia Plath, Leeds University Union Theatre Group

Time of the Season (n) by Mike Pearson, Llanover Hall Theatre Workshop, Cardiff

Tom Thumb by Henry Fielding, UKC Dramatics, University of Kent, Canterbury

Trilogy (d) Royal School for the Deaf, Derby

You Must Be Mad (d) including The Blue One (ns) by Angela Farrow (a: Sunday Times Playwriting Award) Entrogs, Coventry College of Education

sp: The Sunday Times; lo: Graham Morris, Shelagh Hendry, Rae Levine & Sue Swift; td: Steve Ottner

1975

Act Without Words by Samuel Beckett, Edinburgh University Theatre Company

Albert's Bridge by Tom Stoppard, Imperial College Dramatic Society

Backlog (ns) by Joe Richards, Hull University Drama Department

A Cage Went in Search of a Bird (ns) by Chris Hauke (ad from Kafka), New College of Speech & Drama

The Chairs by Eugène Ionesco, Drama Department, University College, Aberystwyth

Chicago by Sam Shepard, Nottingham University Drama Society

Chase (ns, d) Framework Theatre, 2nd Year Theatre Design students, Central School of Art & Design

The Franklin's Tale (ns, ad by the company from Chaucer), Wall Hall College, Aldenham

God, Herbert, Donne and the Devil (ns) by Michael Boyd, Edinburgh University Theatre Company (a: Kevin Laffan Mystery Award, Michael Boyd)

Gum and Goo by Howard Brenton, Dunce Theatre, Northampton College of Education

Interview by Jean Claude Van Itallie, Coopers School, Kent

It's Called the Sugar Plum by Israel Horovitz, Manchester Polytechnic Theatre Society

The Labyrinth by Fernando Arrabal, Dublin University Players

Le Piege de Meduse by Satie, Musik Circus, Keele University

The Lion in Winter by James Goldman, Queen's University Belfast Drama Society

Marat/Sade by Peter Weiss, Geoffrey Skelton & Adrian Mitchell, Arts Festival, Theatre Group and Light Opera Soc, Leeds University

The Marriage by Witold Gombrowicz, Bristol University Drama Society

Music Mimes (d) Clarendon College of Further Education

Of the Farm by John Updike (ns ad by Joe Richards), Hull University Drama Department

Oh! Mr Asquith (ns, d) Wall Hall College, Aldenham

People Are Living There by Athol Fugard, Bristol University Drama Department

Prufrock (n) by Edwina Dorman, The Drama Studio, London

Sandpaper (n) by David Savage, Good Words Group, Keele University

Sequel to Jeso by Malcolm Purkey, Consortium of Performing Arts, Keele University

Theatre Piece by John Cage, Musik Circus, Keele University

Waiting for Godot by Samuel Beckett, English Drama Society, Bangor Normal College

Who, Me? by W Gordon-Smith, Edinburgh University Theatre Company

Rosencrantz and Guildenstern are Dead by Tom Stoppard, Dramatic Society, University College, London (nc)

The Man and the Myth (n, d from the work of Dylan Thomas) Revunions, Bristol University (nc)

The Driver's Seat (n) by Una Ponsonby (ad from Muriel Spark), The Barnstormers, Turku, Finland (nc)

The Supper (d) Comuna Teatro de Pesquisa, Lisbon, Portugal (nc)

sp: The Sunday Times; lo: David Cooke & John Parry; td: Paul Adams

1976

Coup d'Etat (n) by Paul Bream, Keele University Drama Group

England October 30th, 1975, (ns, d) Framework Theatre, 2nd Year Theatre Design Students, Central School of Art & Design

Galatea (n) by Jacek Laskowski, Mermaids Dramatic Society, St Andrews University (a: Michael Codron Award)

Gas by Georg Kaiser & J B Kenworthy, Theatre Workshop MA Group, Leeds University (a: Buzz Goodbody Student Director Award, Phil Young)

The Key (ns) by Robert Pugh, Rose Bruford College of Speech and Drama (a: *Sunday Times* Playwriting Award)

Leonardo's Last Supper by Peter Barnes, Strathclyde University Theatre Group

Not I by Samuel Beckett, Strathclyde University Theatre Group

Old Times by Harold Pinter, University of East Anglia Drama Group

Palach by Charles Marowitz & Alan Burns, Durham University Theatre

Play of William Cooper and Edmund Dew-Nevett by David Selbourne, Cambridge University Mummers, Theatre Work Group

Swan Song by Anton Chekhov, St Andrews Mermaids

More than One (ns improvisation), Strathclyde University Theatre Group

The Stormwatchers (n) by George Mackay Brown, Strathclyde University Theatre Group

A Terrible Beauty (n) by Frank Oates, Wakefield Prison (nc)

Yobbo Nowt by John McGrath, 7:84 Theatre Company (nc)

sp: *The Sunday Times*, Scottish Tourist Board, House of Fraser & Scottish Arts Council; lo: Brian Hawkins

1977

Bingo by Edward Bond, ADC, Cambridge University

A Ceremony of Innocence (the birth and death of Jesus Christ) (ns) compiled by Mary Nelson & Judy Ratcliffe, Middlesex Polytechnic at Ivy House

The Dark Tower by Louis MacNiece, Sherman Arena Company, University College, Cardiff

Endgame by Samuel Beckett, Newcastle University Theatre Society

Happy Days by Samuel Beckett, Middlesex Polytechnic at Hendon (a: Buzz Goodbody Student Director Award (joint), Jayne Chard)

Hold Your Horses, Mussolini! (n) by Simon Harries, Students Union, Welsh College of Music & Drama

The Interrupted Act by Tadeusz Rozewicz, 3rd Year Certificate of Education course, Middlesex Polytechnic at Trent Park

King Lear by William Shakespeare, Independent Theatre, Cambridge

King Lear by William Shakespeare, Workshop Theatre, Leeds University

Krapp's Last Tape by Samuel Beckett, ADC, Cambridge University (a: Buzz Goodbody Award (joint), RogerMichell; Best Actor, Alan Barker)

Like Dolls or Angels (n) by Stephen Jeffreys, Carlisle College of Art & Design (a: Best New Play)

Murder in the Cathedral by T S Eliot, Glasgow University Student Theatre Group

The Occultist (ns) by Kevin Buxton, Nottingham University Dramatic Society

The Orange, the Green and the Red, White and the Blue (ns) by David Hornbrook co-written with the company, City of Bath Technical College Drama Department (a: Inter-Action Community Theatre Prize)

The Private Life of Superman (n) by Chris Barlas & Phil Wharton, Bradford University Drama Group

Pushed Into It (ns) by Dave Bell, Durham University Theatre

Rosencrantz and Guildenstern are Dead by Tom Stoppard, Warwick University Drama Society

Rox (ns) by Richard Maher, Cambridge University Mummers

Saturday (ns) by Dave Jacks & Richard Lewis, Bretton Hall College

Split Level (ns) by Iaine Renwick, Cambridge University Mummers (a: *Sunday Times* Playwriting Award)

A Waiting Room (n) by Dave Simpson, Bingley College Students' Union

Wild About Harry (n) by Dave Simpson, Bingley College Students' Union

ISPC, Louise Page, *Lucy*

sp: *The Sunday Times*, Scottish Tourist Board & Scottish Arts Council; lo: Jonathan Glenn; td: Tim Parkin

1978

Abide With Me by Barrie Keeffe, Leeds University Union Theatre Group

Blood Sports by David Edgar, Warwick University Drama Society

The Burning of Carthage (ns d) ad from a story by Ivor Benjamin & Jeremy Monson, ADC, Cambridge University (a: Howard Davies Conditional Prize)

Cycles (ns d) LAMDA (dir Edwina Dorman)

Do Not Tap on the Glass (ns d) Manchester University Drama Department (a: Kenneth Pearson Prize)

Endgame by Samuel Beckett, Bedford College, London University

Entertaining Mr Sloane by Joe Orton, Warwick University Drama Society

Ghosts by Henrik Ibsen, Queen's College, Oxford

If One Green Bottle (ns) by Bill Anderson, Aberdeen University Dramatic Society (a: The Almost Free Theatre's Naftali Yavin Prize, Bill Anderson)

Muggins (ns improvisation) Bosworth College, Leicester (a: The Inter-Action Community Theatre Prize)

Old Man/Telephone (ns d) Manchester University Drama Department

Saved by Edward Bond, Durham University Theatre

Sherlock's Last Case by Matthew Lang, Manchester Umbrella Theatre Company

The White Devil by John Webster, Newcastle University Theatre Society

Who's Afraid of Virginia Woolf? by Edward Albee, Trent Drama Workshop, Middlesex Polytechnic

Acting Shakespeare d & performed by Ian McKellen, special guest performance, proceeds donated to NSDF

Romeo and Juliet by William Shakespeare and **Avram Iancu** (n) by Mihai Manutiu, Institute of Theatrical and Cinematographic Art, Bucharest, Romania (nc)

ISPC, Terri Wagener, *Renascence*

sp: *The Sunday Times*, Granada Television, Hallmark Cards, IBM, London Weekend Television, Thames Television, Anglia Television, Guinness, Pitman Publishing & Margaret Ramsay; lo: Chris Fisher; td: Ken Hall

1979

Anna-Luse by David Mowat, Hull University Drama Department

Christie in Love by Howard Brenton, Newcastle University Theatre Society

The Contrivance (ns) by Tony Browne, New University of Ulster Drama Society

The Day Centre (n) by David Farnsworth, Bretton Hall College

The Glass Menagerie by Tennessee Williams, Dramatic Society, Grey College, Durham University

Gotcha by Barrie Keeffe, Dramatic Society, University College, Swansea

Ivan (ns) by Anthony Clark (based on Tolstoy), Manchester Umbrella Theatre Company (a: Buzz Goodbody Student Director Award (joint), Anthony Clark)

Magnificence by Howard Brenton, Cambridge University Mummers

Marriage by Gogol (tr Bella Costello) Manchester Umbrella Theatre Company

Mr Black's Poems of Innocence (n) by D M Thomas, Southampton University Theatre Group

No Pasaran by David Holman, Drama Society, St Mary's College, Twickenham

Oedipus the King by Sophocles (tr Anthony Burgess), Warwick University Drama Society

Riders to the Sea by J M Synge, Leeds University Workshop Theatre (a: Buzz Goodbody Student Director Award, (joint), Patricia Curran)

Sexual Perversity in Chicago by David Mamet, Edinburgh University Theatre Company

Stageplay (ns) by Oliver Muirhead, Edinburgh University Theatre Company

Tartan (ns) by K W Ross, Cambridge University Mummers (a: *Sunday Times* Playwriting Award)

They Shoot Doughnuts, Don't They? (ns) by Trevor Cooper & Robert Paterson, Peachville Productions, Drama Studio, London

Toys of Age (ns) by Richard Lewis & John Godber, Bretton Hall College

Valley of the Ashes (ns d) Dunce Theatre, Nene College

Woyzeck by Georg Buchner (tr Malcolm Griffiths), Warwick University Drama Society

This End Up (n, d) by Kjartan Poskitt, ex-Durham University (nc)

ISPC, Stephen Lavell, *Had I Been Alone*

sp: *The Sunday Times*, Samuel French, Granada Television, Southern Television, Southern Tourist Board/English Tourist Board, Anglia Television, London Weekend Television, Scottish Television, Southern Arts, Hallmark Cards & IBM; lo: Steve Poulter (a: Michael Imison Student Administrator Award) & Kim Dent; td: Nigel Coopey

1980

The Android Circuit by Tom McGrath, Glasgow University Student Theatre Group

The Caretaker by Harold Pinter, Durham University Theatre

Everyman (anonymous), Royal Holloway College, University of London

Great Expectations* by Charles Dickens (ns ad by the company), Royal Scottish Academy of Music & Drama

I Was A Teenage Prat (ns) by Duncan Gould, Southampton University Theatre Group (a: The Almost Free Theatre's Naftali Yavin Prize (joint), Duncan Gould)

Kafka's Last Request* (ns) by Eric Prince, Bretton Hall College (a: *Sunday Times* Playwriting Award)

Knuckle* by David Hare, Dragon Theatre Company, Welsh College of Music & Drama

Milktrane* (ns) by Andy Maw & James Hampton, University of York Dramatic Society

Noonday Demons* by Peter Barnes, Dramatic Society Grey College, Durham University

The Pearl by John Steinbeck (ns ad by Jane Prowse), Green Room Club, Hull University (a: Buzz Goodbody Student Director Award, Jane Prowse)

Potter's Wheel* (ns) by Shaun Prendergast, Bretton Hall College (a: The Almost Free Theatre's Naftali Yavin Prize (joint), Paul Cowen, dir)

The Raft of the Medusa by Georg Kaiser, Thimble Theatre, Manchester University

The Story of Sister Holy Cross of the Blessed Valley Who Poisoned Twenty-Seven Arabs (ns d) Trinity & All Saints Colleges, Leeds

Sylvia Plath by Barry Kyle, Swansea University Drama Society

Tira by Michael Weller, All Saints College, Middlesex Polytechnic

Two Kinds of Angel by David Edgar, Glasgow University Student Theatre Group

* These six plays, and Angie Farrow's *Privitus, Privitorum, Privet Hedge* (NSTC) and Coarse Acting winner *The Road to Bethlehem* by Kjartan Poskitt transferred shortly after the 1980 Festival to the Old Vic, London, for a fortnight given in gratitude for the NSDF's 25 years' service to the theatre.

ISPC, Trevor Cooper, *Lovers Too*

sp: *The Sunday Times*, Samuel French, Granada Television, Southern Television, Southern Tourist Board/English Tourist Board, Hallmark Cards, IBM, Williams Lea Ltd, Scottish Television & Southern Arts; lo: Steve Poulter; td: Ian Cook

1981

Abide With Me by Barrie Keeffe, Southampton University Theatre Group

The Changeling by Middleton & Rowley, Exeter University Student Theatre

Cramp (n) by John Godber, Minsthorpe High School & Community College (a: *Sunday Times* Playwriting Award; Almost Free Theatre's Naftali Yavin Prize; YTV Award; BP Outstanding Production Award)

Equus by Peter Shaffer, Dunelm Theatre Company, Durham University (a: Best Lighting, John Churchill & Andrew Sanderson; Best Incidental Music; Best Publicity and Artwork, Elisabeth Robinson)

Home Sweet Bloody Home (n) by Richard J Lewis, Aston Comprehensive School, Sheffield

How Does Your Garden Grow? (ns) by Joe Turner, Green Room Club, Hull University (a: NT/BP Student Administration Award, Patricia Tulip; Best Supporting Actress, Eileen Ryan)

In Camera by Jean Paul Sartre, Durham University Theatre

Interview by Jean-Claude van Itallie, Bretton Hall College

Kennedy's Children by Robert Patrick, Westfield College Drama Society, London (a: BP Best Acting Company)

A Portrait of Sarah Siddons by Caroline Pugh, Green Room Society, Hull University (a: BP Best Actress, Rebecca Harbord; Best Design, Joe Turner)

The Silent Woman by Ben Jonson, Manchester Umbrella Theatre Company (a: Buzz Goodbody Student Director Award, Laurence Boswell; BP Best Classic Production Award; BP Best Actor, David Phelan; Best Supporting Actor, Tony Johnson)

Somewhere in Barnet (ns) by Martin Jacobs & Michael Baran, Manchester Umbrella Theatre Company (a: Inter-Action Community Theatre Prize)

Stiffs (n) by Mark Britton, Sussex University Drama Society

Stories, (ns) 2nd Year Theatre Design Dept, Central School of Art & Design

Szabo (ns d), Bath Technical College Drama Students (a: Best Stage Management)

Three Sisters by Anton Chekhov, Durham University Theatre (a: Best Costume, Victoria Penny)

Victoria Wood and The Great Soprendo special guest performance

ISPC, Janice Hally, Glasgow University, *Ready or Not*

Sunday Times Student Drama Critic Award, James MacDonald, North London Polytechnic

sp: *The Sunday Times*, BP, Yorkshire Television, Granada Television, London Weekend Television, Lincolnshire & Humberside Arts, Scottish Television, Yorkshire & Humberside Tourist Board/English Tourist Board; lo: David Hurst; td: Ian Cook

1982

Brenda (ns) by Hugh Charterton & Paul Lister, Manchester Umbrella Theatre Company (a: Best Set Design; Best Lighting Board Operation)

Caesar (ns) by Gerard Maguire, Manchester Umbrella Theatre Company

The Dog in the Manger by Lope de Vega, Manchester Umbrella Theatre Company (a: YTV Award, Laurence Boswell; BP Best Classic Production Award; Best Supporting Actress, Katharine Jones)

EPA (n) by John Godber, Minsthorpe High School & Community College

Faith Healer by Brian Friel, Z Theatre Company, Hull University (a: Best Actress, Eileen Ryan)

The Goalkeeper's Revenge by Ray Speakman & Derek Nicholls (ad from Bill Naughton), Birmingham Youth Theatre (a: Best Company Acting; Best Supporting Actor, George Usill; Best Comedy Performance, Sara Thomas; Best Incidental Music, Sophie Aldred)

Goetz von Berlichingen by Goethe (tr Tony Meech), Hull University Drama Department

Happy Jack (n) by John Godber, Minsthorpe High School & Community College (a: Outstanding Production Award)

Lilliput by David Karp (ad by Nigel Pugh), Sutton Coldfield College of Further Education

Little Grey Man (ns d) Bretton Hall College

Lying Truths (ns d) Bretton Hall College (a: Best Lighting, Ralph Hanes)

The Sabre-Tooth Curriculum (d) by Harold Benjamin, St Luke's College, Exeter (a: Inter-Action Community Theatre Award)

The Seagull by Anton Chekhov (ns tr Nicholas Mahon), University of East Anglia (a: NT/BP Student Administration Award, Lesley Wake)

Small Beginnings (ns) by Jeremy Brock, Bristol University Dramatic Society (a: Buzz Goodbody Student Director Award, Simon Curtis; *Sunday Times* Playwriting Award; Best Actor, Cyril Nri; Best Stage Management)

Through the Iris (ns d) Hull University Drama Department

Voyage Fantastique (ns) by Tim Dodd, Wimbledon School of Art (a: Best Costume, Tim Dodd)

A World of Stone (ns) by Stephen Chambers, Z Theatre Company & Green Room Club, Hull University

ISPC, Mick Yates, West Bridgeford College of Further Education, *Breaks*

Sunday Times Student Drama Critic Award, Robert Randall, Birmingham University

Michael Imison Translation Award, Hettie MacDonald, Bristol University

sp: *The Sunday Times*, BP, Yorkshire Television, City of Hull, Granada Television, LWT & Scottish Television; lo: David Williams; td: Ian Cook

1983

Chapters in the Life of Arthur Harding (ns) by Peter Jukes, Cambridge University Mummers (a: BP Award for Best Lighting, Mike Dewhurst)

Chicago by Kander & Ebb, Birmingham School of Speech Training and Dramatic Art (a: BP Award for Best Comedy Performance, Amanda Dainty & Catherine Terry)

Comedians by Trevor Griffiths, Minotaur Student Theatre Company, University of East Anglia (a: BP Award for Best Supporting Actor, Gary Bowman)

Die Hose by Carl Sternheim (n ad by Jenny Killick, from tr McHaffie), Guildhall School of Music & Drama Student Theatre Society (a: BP Award for Outstanding Production; BP Award for Best Supporting Actress, Catherine Livesey; BP Award for Best Music, Ally Kessler)

Fall of the House of Usher ad by Steven Berkoff from Poe, The Minotaur Student Theatre Company, University of East Anglia

Harry (ns) by Sebastian Baczkiewicz, Wimbledon School of Art (a: BP Award for Best Design, Lorna Nolan)

In the Shadow of the Glen by J M Synge, Cambridge University Mummers (a: Buzz Goodbody Student Director Award, Peter Jukes; BP Award for Best Actress, Joanna Scanlan, BP Award for Best Lighting, Mike Dewhurst)

The Irons (ns) by Tony Grounds, Central School of Speech & Drama

Krapp's Last Tape by Samuel Beckett, Bretton Hall College

One of Us (n) by Jacqui Shapiro, Manchester Umbrella Theatre Company (a: BP Award for Best Solo Performance, Meera Syal)

Paul (ns d), scripted by Kay Mellor, Bretton Hall College

The Same Old Story by Dario Fo & Franca Rame, Z Theatre Company, Hull University

A Tenant for Edgar Mortez (ns) by Simon Donald & Michael Duke, Abattoir Theatre, Aberdeen University (a: *Sunday Times* Playwriting Award)

A Trick to Catch the Old One by Thomas Middleton, Studio Theatre Group, University College, Swansea (a: NT/BP Student Administration Award, Catherine Carnie)

Troilus and Cressida by William Shakespeare, Manchester Umbrella Theatre Company (a: BP Award for Best Actor, Mark Sproston; BP Award for Best Stage Management, Viv Taylor)

Young Hearts Run Free (n) by John Godber, Minsthorpe High School & Community College (a: BP Award for Best Company Acting)

ISPC, Mark Entwistle, Lancaster University, *The Rhubarb Farm*

sp: *The Sunday Times*, BP, Yorkshire Television, Scottish Television, Wakefield NDC, West Yorkshire MCC & Yorkshire Arts Association; lo: Jon Willis; td: Ian Cook

1984

Bread'n'Butter Guns (ns) by Mike Elliston, Red Rose Theatre Company, Lancaster University (a: YTV Award, Mark Elliston)

Christie in Love by Howard Brenton, Manchester Umbrella Theatre Company

Cloud Nine by Caryl Churchill, The Fine Lines Company, Bretton Hall College (a: BP Company Award; BP Technical Award, Phil Summers)

Decadence by Steven Berkoff, No Alternative, Manchester Umbrella Theatre Company (a: BP Acting Award, Denise Evans)

Good by C P Taylor, St Andrews Mermaids (a: BP Acting Award, Mark Walker)

Growing Pains (ns) by Polly Teale, Manchester Umbrella Theatre Company (a: *Sunday Times* Playwriting Award)

Look Back in Anger by John Osborne, Exeter University Student Theatre (a: YTV Award, Alex Renton, dir)

Medea by Olwen Wymark, Theatre Co-op, University College, Swansea

The Merry Wives of Windsor by William Shakespeare, European Theatre Group, Cambridge University (a: BP Music Award, Dan Warburton)

Montaillou (n) by Paul Clements (ad from Emmanuel Le Roy Ladurie), Bretton Hall College

The Odyssey (ns ad from Homer), Anaber Theatre Company, University College, Aberystwyth (a: BP Company Award; BP Acting Award, Gweneth Owen)

Oedipus by Ted Hughes (n ad from Seneca), Bretton Hall College

On the Outbreath (ns) by Nick Phillips, Z Theatre Company, Hull University (a: BP Company Award; BP Music Award, Nick Phillips)

The Plough and the Stars by Sean O'Casey, Manchester Umbrella Theatre Company

Private Wars by James McLure, Guildhall School of Music & Drama Student Theatre Society (a: BP Acting Award, Andrew Baker, Lorin Stewart & Bryan Torfeh; BP Technical Award, Paul Kell)

Simple Games (n) by Jane Thornton, Minsthorpe High School & Community College

Tracks (n, d), Splash Theatre, Bretton Hall College (a: NT/BP Student Administration Award, Patrick Murphy; BP Company Award)

A Twist of Lemon (ns) by Alex Renton, Exeter University Student Theatre

ISPC, Richard Sinnott, Sutton Coldfield College of Further Education, *Laid on a Pebble Bed*

Sunday Times Student Drama Critic Award, Dion Reilly, Exeter University, Pete Bradshaw, Cambridge University & Lindy Watson, Middlesex Polytechnic

sp: *The Sunday Times*, BP, Yorkshire Television, Scottish Television, Wakefield NDC & West Yorkshire MCC; lo: Patrick Murphy; td: Nick Hunt

1985

Best Man Dead (n, ad from Raymond Briggs), Bretton Hall College

The Crucible by Arthur Miller, Manchester Umbrella Theatre Company

Cupboard Man (n) by Julia Bardsley & Phelim McDermott (ad from Ian MacEwan), dereck, dereck productions, Middlesex Polytechnic (a: Buzz Goodbody Student Director Award, Julia Bardsley; BP Acting Commendation, Phelim McDermott; BP Technical Award)

Dangerous Altercations (n) by Helen Lonergan, Leicester Polytechnic

The Deceits of Memory by Zeami Motokiyo (n tr & ad John Harris), Hull University Drama Department (a: BP Company Award; BP Music Award, Nick Phillips)

Equus by Peter Shaffer, Bristol University

Haunted Sunflowers (n) by Richard Cameron, Thomas Sumpter Comprehensive School (a: *Sunday Times* Playwriting Award; BP Acting Award, John Walding)

In Loving Memory (n, d), Keppel Company, Dartington College of Arts (a: BP Company Award for Ensemble Work)

Letters Home by Rose Leiman Goldemberg, UCNW, Bangor Drama Department

Miss Julie (n, ad from August Strindberg), Swansea University College

Moskva-Petushki by Benedict Erofeev (ad from tr J R Dorrell), Shriek Factory, Bretton Hall College

Nam (n, ad by Mike Baker), Cambridge University Mummers

Now You See Me (n) by Polly Teale, Manchester Umbrella Theatre Company

The Pope's Gig (n) by Eoghan Harris, Communications Department, Dublin College of Commerce (a: NT/BP Student Admin Award, Martha O'Neill)

A Rose on the Obverse (n) by Timothy Jackson, St Andrews Mermaids

Silent Night (n) by Polly Teale, Minsthorpe High School (a: BP Acting Award, Adele Shaw)

Welcome Home by Tony Marchant, Manchester Umbrella Theatre Company

Woyzeck by Georg Büchner, Bristol University, (a: BP Technical Commendation)

Sunday Times Student Drama Critic Award, Nick Phillips, Hull University, Katherine Way, Cambridge University

Michael Imison Translation Prize, Steven Wright, Manchester University

ISPC, Andrew John Stables, Coleg Harlech, *Jack the Lad*

sp: *The Sunday Times*, BP in Wales & Swansea City Council; td: Catherine Carnie & Nick Hunt; lo: Patrick Murphy & Bubble Lodge

1986

Approaching the Traps (n) by Karen Peters, RAP, Roehampton Institute

Breaking the Ice (ns) by Jeremy Brock, BAD Theatre Company, Bristol University (a: BP Acting Commendation, Sean Pertwee)

Diary of a Madman by Robert Waite (n ad from Nikolai Gogol), Simply Now, Middlesex Polytechnic

The Ghost Sonata by August Strindberg (n tr William Woods), Bristol Revunions (a: BP Company Commendation)

In Search of the Almighty (n) by H A Naylor, University College, London

Lone Star by James McLure, Guildhall School of Music & Drama Student Theatre Society

The Lost Giro (n) by James O'Brien, Drama Inc, Polytechnic of Wales (a: *Sunday Times* Playwriting Award; BP Company Commendation)

The Marriage of Heaven and Hell (ad from William Blake by the company), Cambridge Mummers / DIY Theatre Company

My Forgotten Man (d) No Deposit No Return, Shena Simon College Manchester

My Friend Julie (n) by John Herriman, Roade Comprehensive School (a: BP Acting Commendation, Julie Barwick & Gina Lander)

One Fine Day (n) by Eric Prince, North Riding College

The Piper's Song (n) by Phil Blundell & Dave Hirons, Stringer Youth Theatre, Coventry (a: BP Company Commendation)

The Rape by Franca Rame, tr Roger McAvoy & Anna Maria Guigni, University College, Swansea Drama Section

Savage/Love by Sam Shepard & Joseph Chaikin, Westfield College, London

Saved by Edward Bond, Manchester Umbrella Theatre Company

Skylark (ns) by Jonathan Lewis & Jason Carr, Guildhall School of Music & Drama Student Theatre Society

Sour Grapes (ns, revue) by Richard Thomas & Rob Millner, Foot & Mouth, Cambridge University

Under Control (n) by Andrew Plaice, Bacarat Theatre, Crewe & Alsager College

Whistle Daughter Whistle (n, d), Composition IV, Loughborough University

Who's Afraid of Virginia Woolf? by Edward Albee, Tack City, Bretton Hall College (a: BP Acting Commendation, Peter Price)

Sunday Times Student Drama Critic Award, Katherine Way, Cambridge University

ISPC, Kwame Boakye, *Jacob's Ladder*

sp: *The Sunday Times*, BP in Wales, Swansea City Council & HTV Wales; lo: Catherine Carnie, Rick Locker, Patrick Murphy & Michael Simmons; td: Simon Mills

1987

American Eagle (n, d) Bretton Hall College (a: Judges' Company Commendation)

Bazaar and Rummage by Sue Townsend, Bretton Hall College

Beowulf (n, d) Phil Jackson & Steve Hammond, Leicester Polytechnic (a: Buzz Goodbody Student Director Award, David Williams; Judges Acting Commendation, Phil Jackson)

Blind Man's Buff (n) by Beverley Newns, Paradox Theatre Company, University College, Swansea

Closed Doors (d) Shena Simon College, Manchester

Cold Shelter (n) by Orit Azaz, Bristol University Revunions

Count Rakowsky and the Zagrobki Mime Troupe (n) by Michael Wickerek, Theatre of Poland Touring Company (a: Judges' Company Commendation)

The Difference (n) by Neil Filby, Z Theatre Company, Hull University

Holiday in the Sun (n) by Tony Grounds, King Alfred School, Hampstead (a: Judges' Company Commendation)

A Lonesome Road (n, d), Shelley High School

The Same Old Story by Dario Fo & Franca Rame (tr Margaret Kunzle), Female Parts Theatre Company, Middlesex Polytechnic (a: Judges' Acting Commendation, Lois Norman)

Spring Awakening by Frank Wedekind (tr Edward Bond), Worcester Swan Youth Theatre

Statements After an Arrest Under the Immorality Act by Athol Fugard, Westfield College Theatre Company

Torch Songs by Harvey Fierstein, Bretton Hall College

The Venetian Twins by Carlo Goldoni (n tr Anna Farthing), Bristol University Drama Society

Sunday Times Student Drama Critic Commendation, Robert Noble, Hull University, Simon Reade, Exeter University

ISPC, Andrew John Stables, *Two Short Planks*

sp: *The Sunday Times*, City of Wakefield MDC, Yorkshire Television, Yorkshire Arts & IBM; lo: Rick Locker (a: NT/BP Student Administration Award); td: Nick Tobin

1988

The Breakdown (n) by Stewart Harcourt, Mark Jones & Martin Lowe, Hull University Drama Department (a: Judges' Award for Original Conception, Mark Jones)

Cement by Heiner Muller, One Step Theatre Company, Middlesex Polytechnic

Damage Your Children (n, d) STA Travel Theatre Company, Bretton Hall College

The Dresser by Ronald Harwood, STA Travel Theatre Company, Bretton Hall College (a: Judges' Acting Commendation, Paul McCrink)

for colored girls who have considered suicide / when the rainbow is enuf by Ntozake Shange, Barking College of Technology (a: Judges' Award for Best Ensemble)

The House of Bernarda Alba by Federico Garcia Lorca, Cambridge University Mummers

It's Tough on the Streets by Andy Parsons & Henry Naylor, Kiss My Mate, Cambridge

Like a Chicken with No Head (n, d) by Steven Morgan & Mark Waddell, Leicester Polytechnic

A Mad World, My Masters by Barrie Keeffe, Drama Department, UCNW, Bangor (a: Judges' Acting Commendation, Eunice Faulkner)

The Normal Heart by Larry Kramer, Preston Society, Cambridge University

Orphans by Lyle Kessler, North Chadderton School Stage Society (a: Judges' Award for Acting, Matthew Dunster, Allan Hardman & Paul Hilton)

Plaza Suite by Neil Simon, STA Travel Theatre Company, Bretton Hall College (a: National Theatre Student Administration Award, Nick Tobin)

Sister Mary Ignatius Explains it All for You (n) by Christopher Durang (ad by Pamela Campion), Royal Holloway College

Stags and Hens by Willy Russell, North Chadderton School Stage Society

Tales from the Juniper Bowl (n) by Paul Bond, STA Travel Theatre Company, Bretton Hall College

The Tempest by William Shakespeare, Swansea University Players

Trafford Tanzi by Claire Luckham, Cambridge Youth Theatre (a: Judges Commendation for Wrestling Coaching, Neil Sands; Judges' Acting Commendation, Nick Cavaliere)

Twelfth Night by William Shakespeare, Newcastle University Theatre Society

Wildsea-Wildsea (n) by Eric Prince, North Riding College (a: *Sunday Times* Playwriting Award; Judges' Award for Outstanding Production; Judges' Acting Commendation, Anna Pangbourne)

The Zoo Story by Edward Albee, Hull University Drama Department

Miles and Milner (cabaret), Cambridge University (nc)

Sunday Times Playwriting Award, Richard Cameron, Thomas Sumpter School, *Strugglers* (not performed)

Sunday Times Student Drama Critic Award, Michelle Read, Middlesex Polytechnic, Rick Bridge, Cambridge University

ISPC, Katy Dean, Leicester Polytechnic, *Tommy's Girl*

sp: *The Sunday Times*, Judith E Wilson Fund, Colleges of Cambridge University & Eastern Arts; lo: Jane Hepper & Carol-Anne Upton; td: Maya Campbell

1989

Brimstone and Treacle by Dennis Potter, Underground Theatre Company, Durham University

Comedians by Trevor Griffiths, University College, London (a: National Theatre Student Administration Award, Kirsty Dias)

The Curse of Usher (n) by Richard F Green & Thom Strid, Northern Theatre Company Youth

Darkle (n) by Bill Gallagher, Minotaur Student Theatre Company, University of East Anglia (a: *Sunday Times* Playwriting Award; Judges' Acting Commendation, Martin Belville)

Death Warmed Up (ns) by Mark Gatiss & Steve Pemberton, Mandy Theatre Company, Bretton Hall College

The Disappeared (n) by Paul Toolan (ad from poems by Ariel Dorfman), Clarendon College, Nottingham University

Extremities by William Mastrosimone, LAMP Productions, Cambridge University

Godspell by John Michael Tebelak & Stephen Schwarz, Roade School (a: Publicity Award; Judges' Company Award)

Harold's Day (n) by Tim Fountain, Z Theatre Company, Hull University

A Kind of Alaska by Harold Pinter, Ears of the Groundlings, Birmingham University (a: Judges' Acting Commendation, Emma Hutson)

King Lear by William Shakespeare (shortened), Oxford University Drama Society (a: Judges' Company Commendation)

King Ubu by Alfred Jarry, St Andrews Mermaids

Metamorphosis by Steven Berkoff, St Andrews Mermaids

The Moon's the Madonna (n) by Richard Cameron, Thomas Sumpter School (a: Judges' Company Award; Judges' Acting Award, David Newborn)

Now is the Time… (n) by David Bridel, Z Theatre Company, Hull University

The Ode to St Cecilia (n) by Steve Shill & Matt Wicks, Leicester Polytechnic (a: The Royal Insurance Award for Outstanding Contribution to the Festival)

The Queen's Shilling by Brian Ashton, West London Institute of Higher Education

Road by Jim Cartwright, Given Time Theatre Company, Bretton Hall College

Shakers by John Godber & Jane Thornton, Homerton College, Cambridge University

Subject to Change (n, d), Flopniknotch Theatre Company, Middlesex Polytechnic

Where the Wild Things Go (d), additional writing by Ewan Foster, Theatrestop, Dartington College

Kiss My Mate (n, cabaret), Henry Naylor & Andy Parsons

Sunday Times Student Drama Critic Award, Ian Shuttleworth, Cambridge University

ISPC, Biyi Bandele-Thomas, Awolowo University of Benin, Nigeria, *Rain*

sp: *The Sunday Times*, Judith E Wilson Fund, ITV & Eastern Arts; lo: Jane Hepper (a: National Theatre Student Administration Award) & Carol-Anne Upton; td: Stephen Christopher

1990

Agamemnon by Steven Berkoff, Birmingham Rep Youth Workshop (a: Judges' Company Commendation)

Backbone (n) by Michelle Jones, Corkscrew Theatre, Bishop Grosseteste College (a: Judges' Acting Commendation, Michelle Jones)

The Big Book for Girls (n, d) by Joe Richards, Dartington College of Arts (a: National Theatre Student Administration Award, Paula McFetridge; Judges' Company Commendation)

Can't Stand Up for Falling Down (n) by Richard Cameron, Thomas Sumpter School & John Leggott College (a: *Sunday Times* Playwriting Award; Judges' Acting Commendation, Joanne Wootton)

The Changeling by Middleton and Rowley, Merton Floats, Oxford University Drama Society

Cold Comfort (n, d), Silver Arcade, Leicester Polytechnic

Futurist Love in the Apple (n) by David Bridel, Z Theatre Comapany, Hull University (a: Royal Insurance Award for Outstanding Company Contribution to the Festival; Judges' Award for Best Costume Design, Dulcie Best)

The Hypochondriac by Alan Drury & Justin Chadwick (ad from Molière), Silver Arcade, Leicester Polytechnic

Introcuing Andre Boloque (n, cabaret), Andrew Clover (nc)

Look Back in Anger by John Osborne, Guernsey Youth Theatre

Love Kevin (n) by Richard F Green, Thom Strid & Jonathan Holtby, Northern Theatre Company

Morning Has Broken (n) by Tim Fountain, Z Theatre Company, Hull University (a: Judges' Acting Commendation, Polly Freeman)

Nevim Kudi Kam (I Don't Know Where I'm Going) (n) by Lenka Lagranova, The Academy of Performing Arts, Damu, Prague (nc)

On Hamlet ad from William Shakespeare by David Farr, Panic Theatre, Cambridge University (a: Judges' Acting Commendation, Ben Miller)

Radio Man (n, d), Head First Theatre Company, Middlesex Polytechnic

Spring Awakening by Frank Wedekind, Ursa Minor Company, Roehampton Institute

Introducing André Boloque (m, cabaret), SPOT Theatre Company, Cambridge University (nc)

Sunday Times Student Drama Critic Award, Adam Craig, Exeter University

ISPC, Ndubuisi Anike, University of Benin, Nigeria, *Catalyst of the New Dawn*

Judges' Technical Commendation, Catherine Robertson, North Riding College

sp: *The Sunday Times*, ITV, Scarborough Borough Council, Royal Insurance, British Gas, NatWest, Scarborough & The Ward Group; lo: Matthew Hansell; td: Stephen Christopher

1991

Blue (n) by Michelle Jones, Corkscrew Theatre, Bishop Grosseteste College

Bouncers by John Godber, Increasingly Important Theatre Company

The Coca-Cola Dragon (n) by Steven Downs, Shelley High School

Flesh and Bone (n, d), Lancaster University Theatre Group

In the Ruins of Song (n) by Eric Prince, North Riding College

Judging Billy Jones by Les Smith, Young Company, Young Vic (a: Judges' Company Award)

Low Level Panic by Clare McIntyre, Z Theatre Company, Hull University (a: Smith College (USA) Award for Outstanding Female Contribution to the Festival)

Making the Number Up (n, d) by Stranmillis College, Belfast (a: Royal Insurance Award for Outstanding Contribution to the Festival; Judges' Company Award; Judges Commendation for Design, Heather Wedlock)

Morons (n) by Alan Brookes, Trinity Theatre Group, Warwick (a: Judges' Company Award)

Neurotic Norman (n, d), Bretton Hall College

No Tender Vocabulary (n, d) by Bob Leaver, Bretton Hall College

Pinocchio by Ben Benison (ad from Carlo Collodi), Birmingham Rep Youth Workshop

Play for Yesterday by James Saunders, Corkscrew Theatre Company, Bishop Grosseteste College

The Real McCoy (n) by Phil Higginson, Guernsey Youth Theatre

Rule 43 (Disappear Here) (n, d), Leicester Polytechnic

The Transfiguration of Benno Blimpie by Albert Innaurato, Bretton Hall College (a: Judges' Company Award)

Sunday Times Student Drama Critic Award, Andrew Clover, Oxford University, Donna Munday, Lancaster University

ISPC, Vanessa Alexander, University of Otago, New Zealand, *My Nightingale's Come Unzipped*

sp: *The Sunday Times*, ITV, Scarborough Borough Council, Smith College, USA & Yorkshire Arts; lo: Matthew Hansell (a: National Theatre Student Administration Award); td: Stephen Christopher

1992

Accidental Death of an Anarchist by Dario Fo with additional material by Paul Arendt, Ian Tayor & Hannah Boucher, Guernsey Youth Theatre

The Crucible by Arthur Miller, Youth Theatre, Young Vic (a: Judges' Acting Award, Jud Charlton)

Face To Face (n, d), Fecund Theatre, Bretton Hall College (a: Best Devised Work; Commendation for Costume, Pippa Bound & Clare Morgan)

Goddess (n) by Kirsty Peart, BATS, Cambridge University (a: Commendation for Dancing, Gabriella Chidgey)

Jekyll and Hyde (n, d, ad from R L Stevenson), Bretton Hall College (a: Commendation for Ensemble Work)

Living by Numbers (n) by Louise Jones, Leicester Polytechnic (a: The Outstanding Work of the Festival Award; Commendation for Direction, Kevin Dawson; Smith College (USA) Award for Outstanding Female Contribution to the Festival, Louise Jones)

Many Rivers (n) by Steven Downs, Shelley High School (a: Commendation for Live Music, The Steel Band)

A Nation Not So Blessed (n, d), Bare Faced Ensemble, Middlesex Polytechnic

Not Not Not Not Not Enough Oxygen by Caryl Churchill, Distant Thunder Theatre Company, Central School of Speech & Drama (a: Commendation, Technical Team & Lana Snook)

Return of the Ashplant Hero (a new James Joyce music play) by Ita O'Donnell, Bath College of Higher Education (a: Commendation for Singing, Elizabeth King)

Ruddigore by Gilbert & Sullivan, St Mary's Roman Catholic High School, Tyldesley, Manchester (a: Best Production of the 1992 Festival; Judges' Acting Award, Phillipa May; Commendation for Acting, Jill Tryner)

They Shall Not Grow Old (n) by Gary Drabwell, Bedfordshire City Youth Theatre

Two Into One (n) by Marcus Lund & Dave Gill, Carpe Diem Theatre Company (a: Best Collaboration by a New Company)

Who? (n) by Kevin Tomlinson, Kepow Theatre Company, Hull University (a: *Sunday Times* Playwriting Award; Commendation, David Brown; Publicity Award)

Kukutyne by Marcelijus Martinaitis, Courtyard Theatre, Vilnius University, Lithuania (nc)

Sunday Times Student Drama Critic Award: Robert Shearman, Exeter University

ISPC, Robert Shearman, Exeter University, *Couplings*

sp: *The Sunday Times*, BBC, Scarborough Borough Council, Kodak Ltd-Copier Division, Smith College, USA & Yorkshire & Humberside Arts; lo: Libby Peat (a: National Theatre Student Administration Award); td: Steve Ingham

1993

Blood Wedding by Federico Garcia Lorca, European Theatre Group, Cambridge University (a: Commendation for Music, Loz Kaye)

Chunnel of Love (n) by Mark Wheeller & Graham Cole, Oaklands Youth Theatre, Southampton

Easy Laughter (n) by Robert Shearman, Exeter University Theatre (a: *Sunday Times* Playwriting Award; Commendation for Acting, Philip Wolff & Jessica Willcocks)

Face Licker Come Home by Rita Ann Higgins, Stranmillis College, Belfast

For Grandparents Everywhere (n, d) Department of Performing Arts, De Montfort University (formerly Leicester Poly)

Meshe (n) by Karen Whiteley, Carpe Diem Theatre Company, Leeds

The Odyssey by Homer (n ad by Steven Downs), Shelley High School (a: Commendation for Disciplined Group Creativity)

Ripley Bogle by Robert McLiam Wilson (ad by Richard Hurst), Littlewit Theatre Company, Oxford University (a: Commendation for Acting, Michael Hughes)

Road by Jim Cartwright, University of Derby Drama Society (a: Award for Total Theatre)

Sandcastle (n) by Andrew Wilford, University College, Scarborough (a: Buzz Goodbody Student Director Award, Andrew Wilford)

Séance (n) by Eric Prince, University College, Scarborough

Still Life by Noel Coward, CADS, Cambridge University (a: Award for Direction, Tom Smith; Award for Acting, Anna Thomas)

Talking Birds (n) by Alexandra Tolk, Talking Birds Theatre Company, Warwick University (a: Award for Total Theatre; Publicity Award)

Translations by Brian Friel, Glasgow University Theatre

Miles and Millner revue (nc)

ISPC: Esiaba Irobi, Leeds University, *Cemetery Road*

Smith College (USA) Award for Outstanding Female Contribution to the Festival: Aileen Gonsalves, Central School of Speech & Drama

National Theatre Student Administration Award: Abigail Anderson, Oxford University

sp: *The Sunday Times*, BBC, Scarborough Borough Council, Arts Council GB, Kodak Ltd-Copier Division, Smith College, USA & IBM; lo: Donna Heppenstall; td: Matt Kneeshaw

1994

The Bacchae (n) by Rosanna Lowe (ad from Euripides), Flesh & Blood Theatre Group, Cambridge University

Circles (n) by Steven Downs, Shelley High School, Huddersfield

East by Steven Berkoff, Strange Fish, Cambridge University

Equus by Peter Shaffer, Brouhaha Theatre Company, Queen Mary and Westfield College

Fire-Escape (n) by Andrea Dougherty, Stranmillis College Theatre Company (a: Smith College (USA) Award for Outstanding Female Contribution to the Festival, Andrea Dougherty)

Giovanni's Women (n) by R D Hamilton, So Soo Me Theatre Company, East 15 Acting School (a: Company Commendation for Production Craft; Performance Commendation, Susan Arnold)

Glengarry Glen Ross by David Mamet, Bretton Hall College (a: Performance Commendation, Mike Chapman)

Going Up (n, d) music and lyrics by Loz Kaye, Flesh & Blood Theatre Group, Cambridge University (a: Company Award for Vision and Risk)

Jack (n) adapted from David Greenspan's script, Centre for Media, Performance & Communications, University College, Salford (a: Company Award for Impact and Invention)

Oedipus Tyrannos by Sophocles (tr Timberlake Wertenbaker), Wirral Metropolitan College

The Paradise Maker (n) by Philip Keenan, Goldsmiths College, London

She'll Be Coming Round the Mountain (n, d) BackStairs Influence, Middlesex University (a: Award for Performance, Emma Powell & Jason Thorpe; Company Award for Imagination and Outstanding Performance)

Sumidagawa by Yuro Motomasa / **Purgatory** by W B Yeats, Minotaur, University of East Anglia (a: Design Commendation, Jo Fletcher)

A Summer's Day by Slawomir Mrozek, Rose Bruford College

Why is John Lennon Wearing a Skirt? by Claire Dowie, Split Vision, University of Kent, Canterbury

ISPC, David Wareham, *Fortunes*

Sunday Times Harold Hobson Student Drama Critic Award: Richard Hurst, St Hugh's College, Oxford

Sunday Times Student Drama Critic Award: Charlotte Harris, The Mount School

sp: *The Sunday Times*, BBC, Scarborough Borough Council, Arts Council GB, Kodak Ltd-Copier Division, Smith College, USA & IBM; lo: Cheryl Govan; td: Jo Horrobin

1995

Desert Island Dream Girl (n) by Robert Hamilton, So Soo Me Productions, East 15 Acting School (a: *Sunday Times* Playwriting Award)

Flatmates (n) by Sarah Nelson, Department One Theatre Company, Central School of Speech & Drama

For Those Who Eat the Yellow Snow and the Liquorice Between their Toes (n) by Mette M Bølstad, B & B, Central School of Speech & Drama (a: Personal Managers Association Award, Mette M Bølstad; Acting Commendation, John Herbert)

Greek by Steven Berkoff, In Your Space Productions, Leeds University

Kiss, Cuddle or Torture (n) by Paul Telfer, Phoenix Theatre, Yarm School

Let's Play a Game Called Sorry (n) by Lynn Jefferson, UGly Productions/Stolen Art Theatre Company, University of Glamorgan (a: Company Award; Acting Commendation, Emily McKenzie)

Madwoman in the Attic (n) by Jacqueline Haigh, Keble College, Oxford

The North Pole (n) by Benedict Cooper, AMEN Theatre Company, Rose Bruford College of Speech & Drama (a: Company Commendation)

Pericles: Prince of Tyre by William Shakespeare, Red Rose Chain Theatre Company, Ipswich

Right to Silence (n) by Greg Jemison, Headlands Theatre Workshop, Headlands School, Bridlington (a: Company Commendation)

State of Decay (d) by Anthony Preston & Nick Maynard, Burnley Youth Theatre (a: Company Commendation)

Thinking of You (n) by R Fears & M Chapman, Duped, Bretton Hall College

To Comfort Ghosts (n) by Simon Glass, The GlassCake Theatre Company, Hull University (a: Company Commendation)

Violent Night (n) by Kenn Price & Richard Hurst, Absinthe Theatre Company, Welsh College of Music and Drama (a: Buzz Goodbody Student Director Award, Richard Hurst; Acting Commendation, David Little & Griffin Price)

The Zoo Story by Edward Albee, Gettey Theatre Company, Bretton Hall College

Soundjata (n, d) University of Cape Town Drama Department (nc)

Sunday Times Harold Hobson Student Drama Critic Award, Paul Arendt, Bretton Hall College

ISPC, Nick Joseph, Exeter University, *The Dead Land*

Festival Director's Award (for Services to Educational Drama), Steven Downs, Shelley High School

sp: *The Sunday Times*, BBC, Scarborough Borough Council, Arts Council of England, Kodak Ltd-Office Imaging & IBM; lo: Eve Franklin-Smith (a: RNT Student Administration Award); td: Jo Horrobin

1996

All the World's a Biscuit (n) by Tim Glover, Garibaldy Productions, Hull University (a: Award for Originality and Completely Off-The-Wall Lunacy, Tim Glover)

The Backyard Miracle (n, d), Suitcase Theatre Company, Birmingham University

The Bald Prima Donna by Eugène Ionesco, Garibaldy Productions, Hull University (a: Directing Award, Claire Marie Prenton; Acting Award, Sam Troughton; Design Commendation, Ruth Paton)

Beautiful Thing by Jonathan Harvey, Barking Mad Theatre Company, Bretton Hall College (a: Company Commendation)

Cabaret by Kander & Ebb, UKC Dramatics

The Danube by Maria Irene Fornes, Fall Out Theatre Company, Manchester Metropolitan University (a: Directing Award, Emma Hewitt)

Femme Fatale by Debbie Isitt, Stolen Art, University of Glamorgan (a: Acting Award, Dee Brophy)

Ghetto by Joshua Sobol, Warwick University Drama Society (a: Company Commendation)

Hamlet by William Shakespeare (n ad by Nathan Evans), Oxford University

The Interview and **The Trembling Game** (n) by Robert Hamilton, So Soo Me, East 15 Acting School (a: *Sunday Times* Playwriting Award; Acting Commendation, Suzanne Dawson)

Jamie (n) by Jeanne Kelly & Sarah Gibson, Birchwood High School, Bishops Stortford

Measure for Measure by William Shakespeare (ad by Paul Arendt), Holy Cow Productions, Bretton Hall College (a: Directing Commendation, Paul Arendt)

Our Gang by Eric Bogosian, Welsh College of Music & Drama

The Politics of Altitude (n) by Colin Muir, Aspects Theatre Company, University College, Salford

Someone Who'll Watch Over Me by Frank McGuinness, Endymion Theatre Company, LIPA

Strong Family Values (n) by Richard Hurst & Oliver Matthews, Welsh College of Music & Drama

ISPC, Richard Dingwall, Otago University, New Zealand, *The No Men*

Sunday Times Harold Hobson Student Drama Critic Award, Anya Sen Pearse, West Herts College, Watford

Festival Director's Award (for outstanding services to the NSDF and NSTC over 15 years), Steve Garrett

sp: *The Sunday Times*, BBC, Scarborough Borough Council, Arts Council of England, Kodak Office Imaging & IBM; lo: Louise Hazell & Sarah Nicholson (a: RNT Student Administration Award); td: Mark Griffith

1997

A Short Play About Sex and Death (n) by John Donnelly, In Your Space Theatre Company, Leeds University (a: *Sunday Times* Playwriting Award; Personal Managers' Association Award, John Donnelly; Acting Award, Jim Gitsham & John Hopkins)

Amlodi's Journey by Runar Gudbrandsson (d) De Montfort University (a: Commendation for Teamwork, Technical Presentation and Use of Space)

Angels in America by Tony Kushner, Warwick University Drama Society (a: Acting Commendation, Chris Walters)

The Caretaker by Harold Pinter, Slight Pause Theatre Company, Bretton Hall College (a: Buzz Goodbody Student Director Award, Paul Cooke; Acting Award, John McGuiness & Gavin Turnbull)

Decadence by Steven Berkoff, Conspiracy Theatre, Leeds University (a: Ensemble Acting Award, Kayla Fell & Nathan Rimmell)

Ground Control (n) by Charlotte Harris, Minotaur Theatre Company, University of East Anglia

Heavy Breathing (n) by Dylan Ritson, Crazy Horse Theatre Company, Cambridge University (a: Acting Commendation, Dan Bates)

Jester (n) by Luke de Woolfson & Jascha Elliott, Vicious Theatre Company, Middlesex University

Lear's Daughters by The Women's Theatre Group & Elaine Feinstein, Victoria Sponge Theatre Company, Manchester Metropolitan University (a: Commendation for Concept and Ensemble)

Mary/Martin by Ellen Chadwick (ad from Rose Tremain's *Sacred Country*), Howl Theatre Company, London

Moby Dick (n, d, ad from Melville), Ten Gallon Theatre Company, Middlesex University (a: Commendation for Teamwork)

Nobody Here But Us Chickens by Peter Barnes, Welsh College of Music & Drama

Not Enough Points on the Chicken (n) by Tim Glover, Bombastic Biscuit Company, Hull University

Two by Jim Cartwright, Guild Theatre Group, Birmingham University

Two by Jim Cartwright, After Hours Theatre Company, Bretton Hall College (a: Ensemble Acting Commendation, Andy Murton & Wendy Reed)

Waiting for Godot by Samuel Beckett, ADC, Cambridge University

Sunday Times Harold Hobson Student Drama Critic Award, Maddy Costa, Cambridge University

ISPC, Tina Westhead, Derby University, *Rotten Apples*

Cheek by Jowl Student Administration Award, Hannah Miller, Hull University

RNT Student Administration Award, Caroline Piggott, Leeds University

Festival Director's Award (for his outstanding contribution to the NSDF and NSTC over many years), Stephen Jeffreys

sp: *The Sunday Times*, BBC, Scarborough Borough Council, Arts Council of England & Danka Office Imaging; lo: Simon Bradshaw; td: Mark Griffith

1998

Aberfan (n) by Mark Jermin, UGly Theatre, Glamorgan University

A-Gender (n, d) Arden Theatre School, Manchester

Ball Boys (n) by David Edgar, The 82 Group, Birmingham University (a: Commendation for Political Theatre)

City Haunts (n, d) ADC, Cambridge University (a: Commendation for Devised Work)

Closer than Ever by Maltby & Shire, Head-to-Toe Theatre Company, LIPA (a: Outstanding Ensemble Award; Performance Award, Louise McCabe)

Dog Eat Dog by Tim Kelly, Endymion Theatre Company, LIPA

The Dwarfs by Harold Pinter, red i production, Welsh College of Music & Drama (a: Performance, Craig Rogan; Commendation for Use of Sound, Bob Fitzgerald)

Guys and Dolls by Jo Swerling, Abe Burrows & Frank Loesser (ad from Damon Runyon) Footlights, Exeter University (a: Award for a Producer, Mo Brindley; Performance Commendation, Iain Potter; Commendation for Choreography, Karen Hall; Commendation for Musical Direction, James Casselton)

Sincerity (n) by Kevin Rundle, Stage to Screen Film & Theatre Society, Warwick University

Stand (n) by David Bown, Northampton College (a: *Sunday Times* Playwriting Award; Outstanding Production Award; Performance Award, Jon France & Tim Page)

The Storyteller (n) by Jit Murad, Ragnarokk Theatre Company, LIPA (a: Performance Commendation, Ashley Alymann)

Terminal by Susan Yankovitz & the Open Theatre Company, ad by Joseph Chaikin and Company, Delaruh, University of Huddersfield

Trainspotting by Harry Gibson (ad from Irvine Welsh), Impact Theatre Company, Halifax School of Integrated Arts, Calderdale Colleges

Under Milk Wood by Dylan Thomas, Gorseinon College

Pidgin Makbed by William Shakespeare (tr into Wol Wantok Pidgin by Ken Campbell), LAMDA (nc)

ISPC, Peter Morris, *The Square Root of Minus One*

Sunday Times Harold Hobson Student Drama Critic Award, Duska Radosvljevic, Huddersfield

Festival Director's Award (for her outstanding contribution to the NSDF and NSTC over many years), Lon David

sp: *The Sunday Times*, BBC Broadcast, Scarborough Borough Council, Arts Council of England & Danka Office Imaging; lo: Joanna Crowley; td: Claudia West

1999

The Absence of War by David Hare, Bristol University Drama Society (a: Buzz Goodbody Student Director Award, Roland Smith; Performance Award, Ben McCann; Commendation For Ensemble Acting)

Beckett Shorts (Act Without Words 1, Breath, Footfalls, Play) by Samuel Beckett, Sheffield University Theatre Company (a: Publicity Award for Promotion before, during and after the Festival)

Come and Go by Samuel Beckett, Paranoia Productions, Blackpool & The Fylde College

Damaged Goods (n) by Steven Talbot, Welsh College of Music & Drama

Einmal ist Keinmal (n, d), imitating the dog, Lancaster University (a: Award for a Devised Piece; Award for Technical Support)

Henna Night (n) by Amy Rosenthal, Seasonal Productions, Birmingham University (a: *Sunday Times* Playwriting Award)

Journey's End by R C Sherriff, Bristol University Drama Society (a: Performance Award, Ollie Walters; Award for Design, Rhian Williams)

Loaded (n) by David Bown, Northampton College (a: PMA Playwright Bursary, supported by The Peggy Ramsay Foundation)

One for the Road by Harold Pinter, Brunel University Music & Drama Society (a: Award for Technical Presentation)

The Problem by A R Gurney Jr., LIPA (a: Award for Generating Theatrical Energy; Commendation for Comedy, Carla MacLean, Ashley Alymann)

A Slice of Saturday Night by The Heather Brothers, Genesis Productions, LIPA (a: Award for Musical Ensemble)

Somogyi's Monologue by Stewart Harcourt, Erroneous Players, LIPA

The Spurt of Blood (n, d) (ad from Antonin Artaud), Seven and My Mate Ken, Bretton Hall (a: Award for Physical Theatre)

Teechers by John Godber, Mosaique, LIPA

These Colours (n) by Nicholas Fieldsend, Organised Anarchy, Middlesex University

A View from the Bridge by Arthur Miller, ADC, Cambridge University (a: Performance Award, Sally Lavelle & Hattie Morahan)

Sunday Times Harold Hobson Drama Critic Award, James Williams, Sheffield University

ISPC, Joey Aucoin & Gloria Calderon, Loyola Marymount University, Los Angeles/Goldsmiths College, London, *Dance Like No-one's Looking*

Festival Director's Award, Iain Ormsby-Knox

sp: *The Sunday Times*, BBC, Scarborough Borough Council, Arts Council of England, Danka Office Imaging & Midland Bank; financially assisted by: The Calouste Gulbenkian Foundation; lo: Ian Morley; td: Claudia West

2000

Agamemnon by Steven Berkoff, Bristol University Drama Department

Can't Stand Up for Falling Down by Richard Cameron, Minotaur, University of East Anglia

Carol Smillie Trashed My Room (n, d), Here Comes Truffle, Middlesex University (a: Award for Design)

Classifieds (n, d) Firsty Work, North West Kent College (a: Commendation for Transcendent Movement)

Counterbalance (n, d) Sheffield University (a: Commendation for Use of Space)

The Hunting of the Snark (ns) by Lu Kemp & Robert Evans (ad from Lewis Carroll), Edinburgh University (a: Cameron Mackintosh Award for Outstanding Contribution to Musical Theatre; Commendation for Ingenuity)

Insomnia (n, d) Warwick University (a: Award for Dance and Physical Theatre; Commendation for Direction, Dominic LeClerc)

The King of Schnorrers by Robert Messik (ad from Israel Zangwill), Labyrinth Theatre, Birmingham University (graduates) (a: Commendation for Storytelling)

The Lion, the Witch and a Bag of Chips (n, d) The Way We Are Over Here, Middlesex University (a: Award for a Devised Piece; Commendation for Individual Performance, Phil Marshall & Audrie Woodhouse)

Marge (n) by Peter Morris, Oxford University Dramatic Society (a: *Sunday Times* Playwriting Award)

Not Him by Howard Barker, Minotaur, University of East Anglia

Silence by Moira Buffini, Welsh College of Music & Drama (a: Buzz Goodbody Student Director Award, Owen Lewis; Commendation for Acting)

Sunnyside by Neill Morton, Lagan College, Belfast (a: Commendation for Ensemble work)

A Trip to Scarborough by Nicholas Phillips (n musical ad from Sheridan), LIPA

Who Wants to Be the Disco King? (n) by Adrian Page, Pear Shaped Productions, Goldsmiths College, London

Words, Words, Words by David Ives, Seasonal Productions, Birmingham University

Sunday Times Harold Hobson Drama Critic Award, Katie Nicholson

Festival Director's Award, Nick Kraven

The Sunday Times, The Mackintosh Foundation, BBC Talent, The Bush Theatre, Danka Office Imaging, HSBC & Arts Council of England; financially assisted by: Scarborough Borough Council & The Calouste Gulbenkian Foundation; lo: Katrina Farrell; td: Chris French

2001

A&R (n) by Peter Morris, Studio Ensemble, Edinburgh University (a: *Sunday Times* Playwriting Award)

Atlantica (n) by Jack Martelli, Pitcairn Drama Company, Cambridge University

Black Boxes and Amber Rooms (n) by Tom Morton-Smith, Minotaur, University of East Anglia

Door 32 (n, d) Scarborough Campus, Hull University (a: Commendation for Style and Impact)

Dystopia (n, d) Warwick University (a: Award for Physical Performance, Helena Sands)

Falsettoland by William Finn, LIPA (a: Buzz Goodbody Student Director Award & Bush Theatre Directing Bursary, Jamie Lloyd; Cameron Mackintosh Award for Outstanding Contribution to Musical Theatre; Commendation for Performance, Emily Dykes)

A Few More Lessons in Love (n, d) Scarborough Campus, Hull University

The Grandmother Project (n) by Jennifer Lindsay, Stanford University (a: Commendation for Creative Endeavour; Commendation for Performance, Emily Dykes)

Judith by Howard Barker, Cambridge University

Junk by John Retallack (ad from Melvin Burgess), Edinburgh University

Pull My Strings (n, d) by Anna Silman & Samuel Booth, York University (a: Award for Craft and Imagination; Festgoers' Award)

Rhian and Ripley (n) by Ashif Verjee, Minotaur Theatre Company, University of East Anglia

Why Wait Til You're Fifty? (n, d) by Robert Collett, DMU Brooksby Melton College

Witness Me (n, d), Halfway Nowhere, Warwick University (a: Award for Physical Theatre; Award for Physical Performance, Helena Sands; Commendation for Lighting, Chris Luffingham)

The Woman Who Walked into Doors (ns) by Liz White (ad from Roddy Doyle), LIPA (a: Award for Best Individual Performance, Liz White; Commendation for Stage Adaptation)

ISPC, Reginald Ofodile, *A Form of Healing*

Sunday Times Harold Hobson Student Drama Critic Award, Dan Bye

Personal Managers' Association Award, Christopher Dunkley, Exeter University

Stephen Joseph Theatre Technical Residency, Neil Hobbes

Royal National Theatre Trainee Producer, Tracey McGarrigan

sp: *The Sunday Times*, BBC Talent, The Mackintosh Foundation, Arts Council of England & HSBC; financially assisted by: Scarborough Borough Council & The Calouste Gulbenkian Foundation; lo: Ian Abbott; td: Chris French

2002

Crave by Sarah Kane, Shoshanah Productions, Oxford University Dramatic Society (a: Cameron Mackintosh Award for Outstanding Contribution to Musical Theatre, Nick Gill; Bush Theatre Directing Bursary & Award for Direction, Lucy Foster)

The Equation of a Child's Laughter (n) by Matthew Richardson, Union Drama Society, Liverpool Hope University

Goes Without Saying (n) by Alison Garner & Di Mahoney, Branch Out Youth Theatre, Cedar School (a: Directors' Guild Award, Rachael Savage; Award for Humanity; Commendation for Performance, Martin Vaughan)

The Hush (ns, d) Nottingham University (a: Festgoers' Award)

I Was Almost Dusty Springfield (n) by Elizabeth Boorman, Loughborough University

Liquid (ns) by Lucy Prebble, Sheffield University (a: Personal Managers' Association Award, Lucy Prebble)

Longwave (n, d) Small Change, Redbourne Upper School (graduates) (a: Award for Innovation)

Mrs Blackwell Eats Her Cake (n) by Ollie Rance, Edinburgh University

Muswell Hill (n) by Tom Green, Oxford University Drama Society (a: *Sunday Times* Playwriting Award)

Notes from Underground by Eric Bogosian, Nigfika, LIPA (a: Buzz Goodbody Student Director Award, Joern-Udo Kortmann; Award for Achievement)

Number 2 (n, d) Brooksby Melton College, De Montfort University (a: Commendation for Dance)

Quirk! (n, d) Brooksby Melton College, De Montfort University (a: Commendation for Dance)

Roberto Zucco by Bernard-Marie Koltes, Hull University Drama Department

Someone Who'll Watch Over Me by Frank McGuinness, St Andrews University

Twenty-two Over Seven (n, d) Contemporary Theatre Project, Scarborough Campus, Hull University (a: Commendation for Collaboration)

Ubu Rex by Alfred Jarry, West Sussex Country Youth Theatre (a: Award for ensemble; Commendation for *Mise en Scene*)

A Woman Alone by Dario Fo & Franca Rame, LIPA

ISPC, Chris Dunkley, *The Devil's Pumpkins*

Sunday Times Harold Hobson Student Drama Critic Award, Dan Bye

Theatre Record Young Drama Critic, Rafael Kingston

Festival Director's Award, Ian Shuttleworth

sp: *The Sunday Times*, The Mackintosh Foundation, Esme Fairbairn Foundation, Arts Council of England, Scarborough Borough Council, The Calouste Gulbenkian Foundation & Foundation for Sport and the Arts; financially assisted by HSBC; lo: Tammy Louise Smith; td: Chris French

2003

1789 by Ariane Mnouchkine, St Paul's Girls School, London

Bedbound by Enda Walsh, Cambridge University (a: Buzz Goodbody Student Director Award & Bush Theatre Directing Bursary, Alex Ferguson; Judges' Award for Acting, Khalid Abdalla & Cressida Trew)

Checkmate (n, d) by Graham Ireland, Brooksby Melton College, De Montfort University

Drip (n, d) Attic People (Lecoq graduates) (a: Judges' Award for Total Ensemble)

The Dudleys (n, d) Liverpool Hope University

The Freudian Slip (n) A Meeting About Laughter, Exeter University (a: Judges' Commendation for Comic Writing; Festgoers' Award)

Heavenly Bodies (n, d) Contemporary Theatre Project, Scarborough Campus, Hull University

Jezebel the Justified (n) by Jonathon Morgan, LIPA

The King of Prussia by Nick Darke, Bristol University Drama Society

The Last Days of Mankind by Karl Kraus, Warwick University

Like Skinnydipping (ns) by Chris Perkin, Edinburgh University (a: *Sunday Times* Playwriting Award; Directors' Guild Award, Chris Perkin)

Macbeth by William Shakespeare, Me Old Chimney Productions (LIPA graduates) (a: Judges' Commendation for Choice of Script)

See You Swoon (ns, d), Deer Park, Dartington College of Arts (a: Stage Electrics Award for Lighting, Tom Kovar; Judges' Award for Best Devised Piece)

A Smile Fell in the Grass (n, d), Bretton Hall College, Leeds University

ISPC, Brian Mullin, *Retrospect*

Personal Managers' Association Award, Ben Richards, Nottingham University, *Cargo* (np)

Sunday Times Harold Hobson Student Drama Critic Award, Ed Lake, Cambridge University

Theatre Record Young Drama Critic, Chris Wilkinson, Cambridge University

Stage Electrics award for Technical Achievement, Katie Hind, Edinburgh University

sp: *The Sunday Times*, The Mackintosh Foundation, Esme Fairbairn Foundation, Arts Council of England, Scarborough Borough Council, The Calouste Gulbenkian Foundation & Noel Coward Foundation; Financially assisted by HSBC; lo: Joanne Murray; td: Katharine Williams

2004

As if a Rag (n, d), Industrial Space, Peterborough Regional College (a: Directors' Guild Award, Rhys McClelland; Stage Electrics Award for Technical Achievement, Ben Hodgekins; Judges' Company Award for Innovation)

Beautiful Thing by Jonathan Harvey, LIPA (a: Stage Electrics Award for Lighting, Julie Kearney; Judge's Individual Award for Acting, Paul Stocker & Kevin Kemp)

Dinner (n, d), Company of Rooks, Leicester College

Greek by Steven Berkoff, Reigate Grammar School (a: Buzz Goodbody Student Director Award, Fiona Clift; Judges' Company Commendation for Ensemble)

The Hamster Theme Park (n, d) Autumn Fish, Goldsmiths College, London (a: Stage Electrics Award for Sound, Theo Sykes & Tim Pickup)

The Laramie Project by Moises Kaufman and the Tectonic Theater, Queen's University, Belfast (a: Bush Theatre Directing Bursary, Des Kennedy; Judges' Company Commendation for Ensemble)

Murmur, BRIT School (a: Judge's Individual Award for Direction, Marcus Condron & Kate Pringle; Judges' Company Award for Ensemble)

Shaking Cecelia (n) by Tiffany Wood & Charlotte Riley, Cat in the Bag, East Durham and Houghall Community College (a: *Sunday Times* Playwriting Award)

Tapped (n, d) Fused Illusion, Hull University (a: Judge's Individual Commendation for Acting, Ed Cobbold & Sophie Dixon; Judges' Company Award for Devised Theatre)

Terrorism by The Presnyakov Brothers (tr Sasha Dugdale), The Laboratory, Birmingham Theatre School

Titus Andronicus by William Shakespeare, Hull University

Unlucky for Some (n, d) Contemporary Theatre Project, Scarborough Campus, Hull University (a: Judges' Company Commendation for Innovation)

Waves (n) Tread Dance Company, Dartington College of Arts (a: Judge's Individual Commendation for Theatrical Exploration, Lisa Bywater & Jenni Malarkey)

Political Assassinator (n, d) Yoram Mosenzon, Dansacademie, Arnhem (nc)

ISPC, Joy Wilkinson, *Interior Design for the Undead*

Sunday Times Harold Hobson Student Drama Critic Award, Chris Wilkinson, Cambridge University

Theatre Record Young Drama Critic, Owen Kingston, York University

sp: *The Sunday Times*, The Mackintosh Foundation, Esme Fairbairn Foundation, Arts Council of England, Scarborough Borough Council, The Calouste Gulbenkian Foundation & Noel Coward Foundation; lo: Joey Holland & Laura Dollimore; td: Katharine Williams

2005

The B File by Deborah Levy, University of Derby

Babel (d) Lewisham College

Bent by Martin Sherman, Queen's University Belfast

The Country Wife by William Wycherley, Rose Bruford

ECIOV (d) Bretton Hall College

Greek by Steven Berkoff, Warwick University

Mikey the Musical (n) by Joel Horwood, UKC Dramatics, University of Kent, Canterbury

Scaramouche Jones by Justin Butcher, Edinburgh University EUTC with Painted Face Productions

Tea Without Mother (d) The Tickling Kitchen, Dartington College of Arts

You Have 10 Minutes (d) Ralph Thoresby High School

Childhood Janacek Academy of Music and Performing Arts, Brno, Czech Republic (nc)

Before Existential Make-over Toneel Academie, Maastricht, Holland (nc)

Was Mona Lisa Una Lampara? BAI Bizkaiko Antzerki Ikastegia, Bilbao, Spain (nc)

Champ/Contre-Champ and **Eleanor!** PARTS Performing Arts Research & Training Studios, Brussels (nc)

This Is Not a Romantic Duet The School for New Dance Development (SNDO), Theatreschool, Hoghschool van de Kunsten, Holland (nc)

ISPC, Jennifer Tuckett, *How to Make an English Heroine*

sp: The Sunday Times, The Mackintosh Foundation, Arts Council of England, Scarborough Borough Council, The Calouste Gulbenkian Foundation, Awards for All & Noel Coward Foundation; lo: Rosemary Manley & James Quaife; td: Anthony Newton

The NSDF welcomes comments on anything in this book, particularly information about early years, factual corrections to this appendix and a more detailed CD. Please write to:

NSDF Office
D14 Foxhole Centre
Dartington
Totnes
TQ9 6EB

e-mail: admin@nsdf.org.uk